Acknowledgements

First, I am very thankful to my guru Shajesh, without whom this chapter of my life would not have happened. I'm grateful to Shajesh for taking me under his wing and including me in his ancient lineage. Shajesh recommended I write this book, and he also gave me permission to release some information about mantras and practices, which was important for me to move forward.

I also must thank my husband, Craig, who has never complained over the years about all of my chanting. He has supported me in writing this book and always believed in me and in this project. Craig was my sounding board on a number of occasions and helped with a last-minute inspiration regarding the title.

Several friends read my manuscript for me early on: Terri del Curto loved the content and took up chanting Om Namah Shivaya right away; Mirakhel Windsong left me innumerable post-it-notes all over my manuscript with many useful comments about grammar, sentence structure, spellings, and ease of understanding; and Shirley Frank, my mother, has been very supportive, and is to be credited with the reason this book has a glossary, which idea she promoted and circled many words in my manuscript that should go in the glossary, among other useful feedback. My thanks to these early readers.

My daughter, Cheryl Walker, an English teacher and a writer herself, gave insightful feedback that caused me to realize the need for a reorganization of chapters, and other useful changes. She and son-in-law Jamshed Jehangir, a lawyer, contributed last minute feedback and some meaningful fine-tuning to help me complete the project. I'm grateful for their love and support.

Rebecca Glenn, yoga student and friend, gave encouragement and some last minute edits. While writers from *Cyberscribes* writing group also contributed some last-minute feedback that helped me wrap up the cover details.

I'm grateful also to everyone who's ever written a book on Hindu or Tantric spirituality in English. Being able to read such books was invaluable to me rounding out my understanding of so many things.

I'd like to thank gurus, yoga teachers, and therapists whose practices and influences affected me in some way. If I were not a yoga teacher, I never would have been online in a yoga forum and found Shajesh. Practices from various disciplines carried me through in life to the place where I finally met Shajesh.

And last but not least I'd like to thank Kundalini Shakti for making this possible, by vivifying my intellect and renewing my creative fire. Without adding this dimension to my experience, I would not have been able to comment in as great a depth as I have.

Contents

TANTRIC JAPA YOGA:

A JOURNEY INTO CHANTING PRACTICES FROM THE AANANDA NATH LINEAGE

By Cathie Frank, M.A.

Preface

I was sitting at my little cube-shaped student desk, in the third grade, hunched forward with my arms on the desk, pencil in hand as Mrs. Moscow gave us each a piece of paper with a squiggly line on it. We were to write a story between one and two pages long about the picture we made out of the squiggly line. I loved this assignment and excelled at it. My desire to write goes back a long way.

In college, with more freedom to pursue independent interests, I took creative writing classes and developed a love of writing poetry. My primary interests began to reveal themselves as writing on the one hand, and spirituality on the other hand. I found the Brotherhood of Life bookstore, across the street from the university campus, and bought myself my first books on spirituality: A book by Baghwan Shree Rajneesh, and two books by Mouni Sadhu (*Concentration* and *Meditation*).

The book by Rajneesh contained thoughtful reflections and the two by Mouni Sadhu had some actual exercises in them: I tried to meditate from the book called "Meditation," sitting in the quaint red velvet chair in my bedroom. I was seated in front of a window, on the second floor, looking out through the top halves of tall, pine trees in the dark, my arms resting on the wooden arm rests in the chair, my feet on the floor. I closed my eyes and breathed quietly, naturally, in the stillness, feeling into the rhythmic flow of my breath in the stillness of night. After a short time, I suddenly felt a strong dizzy sensation move through my head. This startled me and spooked me a little and I ended my meditation abruptly.

The next night I tried again, a simple breathing exercise. I sat cross legged, like a yogi on my bed in the dark, with my bedroom door shut, and meditated. I don't know how long I meditated for, but I had a peaceful feeling and went to bed. I remember as I crawled under the covers, how heavenly the sheets felt; my dull old sheets felt like those of some royalty, and I fell into a quick slumber. I awoke suddenly to find myself in a trance state: my eyes were closed; my body felt like energy was pulsing through it, and I couldn't move; the image of a woman's face flashed before my eyes (somebody I'd never seen before – a blond woman with braids wound in buns over her ears). A little bit of time passed and I was able to move again. However lucid the image was, it seemed sort of random – just a dreamlike flash – and I drifted off to sleep, deciding that I wanted to be a monk when I grew up, and devote myself to meditation. It wasn't the random bit of visual image that made me want to be a monk, but the blissful feelings as I crawled into bed and the experience of a trance state were inklings that there was an inner world waiting to be explored.

Some months later I was in the waiting room to talk to a college counselor and I picked up a magazine from the end table. The magazine had an article about how to do a form of relaxed meditation in a resting position, just mentally relaxing each part of the body, and breathing in a relaxed way. I tried this and I liked it. Now today, as a yoga teacher, I would call this a savasana meditation: savasana is a yoga pose where one rests lying on the back and observes the breath; resting in savasana and observing the breath is the simplest form of meditation there is. I was to do this simple form of meditation often, throughout my early life, and into mid-life. It was relaxing and it was my way to return to my center, letting the business and distraction of a day fall away as the mind settled into repose.

I also tried trataka (gazing) with a candle once. I sat on my bedroom floor in the Luther House, the Lutheran Student Center on campus where I rented a room, and gazed at the candle flame for a while. My breath became calm and even and I had a sort of inner experience that revealed an insight about a deep quality of my personality. As the candle flame flickered gently in my vision, suddenly inner images appeared to me like a dream: first a small bird was flying up so high in the sky, that I was afraid it would lose connection with gravity, get sucked up into the sky, and never be able to fly back down again; then, suddenly, a part of myself was deep under the earth, inside a cave there, hiding away.

I never did the trataka again, although the insight was relevant. It wasn't that I didn't have a positive experience. Maybe at that time in my life I didn't know what to do with the dreamlike images. (Now, looking back, the images seem to contain lucid meaning). The other meditation, resting in savasana, had more practical results: relaxation. The resting meditation would call to me, almost like a bodily urge to eat or sleep. I'd just be so full of any one day and it would call to me to lay down and rest.

As for my studies, I took a couple of poetry writing workshops and found, in poetry, a meditative, creative process that I enjoyed and excelled at. Poetry also had a focus on the inner world and subtle layers of experience. I completed my master's degree in creative writing, and for a short stint after college, tried to get my poems published. I did get a few poems published in literary journals and self-published a little chapbook of my own poems but only had a few copies of it. In fact, I lost interest in writing for many years.

Over the years, my interest in various sorts of spirituality continued. I learned a form of breath meditation that I practiced for some years individually, also meeting for satsangs with a group. Then, in 2014, about two years after becoming a yoga teacher, I met my guru Shajesh in an online yoga group. Shajesh offered to teach me Tantric Japa Yoga. I had no idea at all what this was, but realizing Shajesh was a real tantric teacher and Indian guru, I said "sure!" He gave me my first assignment, and I began to practice it right away. I have been practicing his assignments now for a little over ten years, since July 6, 2014 – I was 51 years old. Now I am 62.

It's been a very interesting ten years, and in the process, alongside doing a lot of Tantric Japa Yoga, I have been living my life. I've been a yoga teacher. I have been reading books, and having my own experiences. Now I have come to a point in my life where I would like to share about my experience studying Tantric Japa Yoga with my guru Shajesh, and all the tantric spirituality I have learned along the way.

I'm also writing this book because I feel our world is evolving fast. Many people are taking up meditation of various sorts, and Hindu Tantric philosophy and practices have a lot to offer. The practices I have learned are useful, in a variety of ways, for a number of reasons, and I want to share an introduction into these practices, along with some elaboration on Hindu Tantric spirituality. And I want to share my own experiences on the path, not just with Tantric Japa Yoga, but in my life, regarding meditation and spiritual experience.

Tantric Japa Yoga is a Hindu Tantric Tradition. There is also Buddhist Tantra, which I know very little about. I will be focusing in this book on Hindu Tantra, and going forward it can be assumed that whenever I use the word Tantra, I mean Hindu Tantra.

Tantra is evolved out of the Vedas and Hindu spirituality and therefore some elements of Hindu thought and belief carry over into Tantra. Referred to by Shajesh as Vedic Tantra, this ancient tantric lineage has a rich store of spiritual practices for the purpose of living a happy life, while enjoying spiritual evolution with the hopes of one day achieving enlightenment.

Tantric Japa Yoga is a system of practices to evolve one's meditation practice over time. It increases in difficulty as one progresses, and evolves various story themes of Hindu Tantric Spirituality. Tantric Japa Yoga is a system of practices for meditation with the goal of activating kundalini so that it rises up and unites with consciousness in the crown, which is called moksha, final awakening, or enlightenment. Tantric Japa Yoga is also a system of learning the spiritual cosmology of the Aananda Nath tantric lineage.

You can do the Tantric Japa Yoga and there is this richness and a complexity that unfolds. Yet it is, all together, as parts of one whole, like beads strung on a necklace. Each bead in its appropriate place, to tell its own part of a story. And it unfolds one's energy. It starts simple and evolves. And it never repeats. The Tantric Japa Yoga system of spiritual unfolding is holistic and well rounded. It includes not just mantras and chanting, but also includes breathing/pranayama practices, dhyana and nyasa. It also incorporates jnana yoga. You can read up on the concepts that are involved in your sadhana (disciplined practice), and that sort of study also contributes to spiritual growth, contributes to meditation, and brings enlightenment.

Tantric Japa Yoga is a system of practices that can carry you far. I have been studying with Shajesh for over ten years now and every forty five days he gives me a new assignment. He never runs out of assignments. There is no repetition of assignments. And the assignments cover everything, from purification practices that involve chanting through the chakras and nyasas or sacred touching, both internal and external. Internal nyasas touch with the imagination on the chakras, part of our inner world – the inner experience. Doing purification practices and practices that work with the chakras also lays the groundwork for kundalini activation and awakening.

You can chant on your own, without a teacher, but it's nice to have a teacher, and even a tantric guru, who can advise you, and if you get into some sort of experience and you have questions, there is somebody who has been through their own journey who is there to guide you.

Shajesh is a very wise and genuine guru and he encourages me to read widely on topics related to Hindu tantric spirituality and religion, and I have done this. There is not much else I can do to make up for the fact that I am a westerner who is studying in America. I am not studying in an ashram in India. I tried to get to an ashram in India once years ago but I was going through a lot at that time in my life and needed to return home. However, now I have my experience with Shajesh, and all that he has taught me has been rich.

Shajesh is a real guru, from an ancient tantric lineage that is thousands of years old, going all the way back to Lord Shiva himself. Shajesh belongs to the ancient Aananda Nath lineage. I was initiated into this lineage when Shajesh gave me his lineage Guru Mantra over ten years ago. The Guru Mantra is a secret mantra that is given from the guru to the disciple, and he has told me that giving me this mantra means I am part of this lineage myself.

That being said, I have to note because it's true: I'm just a student and I never imagined I would ever learn so much Sanskrit chanting. I remember as a new yoga teacher seeing a video on Youtube of a young, five year old, Hindu child singing the Gayatri mantra sweetly. The words rolled off his lips so effortlessly and fluently and I knew in that moment I could never purport to chant mantras unless I had been born and grew up in India, steeped in the culture and like that little child, in a state of innocence the mantra might escape from my lips. I never imagined myself as a westerner, stumbling along through the sacred and foreign sounds. I know many people in the world chant mantras and also many westerners in yoga circles and also people who do this or that meditation program. But this is how I felt about it.

Then I began these practices with Shajesh and I started to make some of the simplest sounds, and I began to learn, and I learned very quickly to appreciate these practices and to see them for what they are: truly a tradition in tantric spirituality.

The Tantric Japa Yoga practices I will share in this book are things I have not seen published on the internet or in books. Some of the things may be familiar, but there is a special formula for the way things are done.

Going forward I will henceforth refer to Tantric Japa Yoga with the abbreviation TJY.

The thing is, in TJY it's not about one individual practice or another. It's about the whole string of practices creating a big picture – an overall effect – and it's about the broader story and the context. It's about growing spiritually.

This is my story of my experience of this tantric tradition and things I have learned along the way. I want to finally share these things in a way that is appropriate to our time, as many people are looking for alternatives. I want to give what I can of this tradition I have learned and continue to learn.

I absolutely know there is so much more to learn and that I will never know it all. There is just too much. I'm here, deep in my western life, living in a bit of a tantric way. And to that end, my Tantra perhaps has a bit of a western flavor to it. Though I practice it as Shajesh gives it to me.

I am ready to share, in the hopes that others who are looking for ways to expand their meditation practices and grow spiritually might find something here they can use.

Of course nobody has to do the exercises, but my hope is that even those who just want to read a book to learn a little more about Tantric Spirituality will feel enriched.

Contact Info:

Shajesh

Email: shajeshtantra@gmail.com

Website: https://www.shajeshtantra.com

Cathie

Email: rioranchoyoga@gmail.com

Website: https://www.rioranchoyoga.com

Part One:
Foundations and Background

Introduction to Part One

Part one of this book is intended to give the reader plenty of foundational and background information.

I begin in Chapter One with a discussion of the guru, and looking back, I see the theme of the guru as the illusive, eternal teacher, woven through my life, although I wasn't thinking in those terms back then. I never really gave much thought to the term guru, and being a westerner, it wasn't part of my thought or vocabulary. If I used the term at all, I would have thought it simply means a person in the world who is sort of like a teacher, who people look up to and respect as a source of knowledge. But I had no immediate connection with any personal guru as a spiritual teacher; I learned more about this later in life, after I met Shajesh. I also explore what it means for me to have a guru in my life.

Chapter One also touches on my evolving spirituality before meeting Shajesh. Our spiritual journeys are unique. There are many paths that are good in their own way. I don't want to give the impression that I just woke up one day and started doing Tantric Japa Yoga in a vacuum. Also, tracing the presence of the guru in various forms in my life and spiritual unfolding is useful as an illustration to the various ways we can experience this concept of the guru.

In Chapter Two, I explore the concept of sadhana, or spiritual discipline, and some related themes. Tantric Japa

Yoga is a form of sadhana. This is related to the tantric goal of raising kundalini in ways that shall reveal themselves as we go.

In Chapters Three and Four, I take the reader on an exploration of the concepts of kundalini and prana, which are forces within us that we strive to activate in Tantric Japa Yoga. Having a deeper understanding of these concepts and how they fit into the big picture, can help us understand and make sense of our practice and its effectiveness in our lives.

With Chapters Five and Six, I explore the idea of chanting – of what it is, its purpose, how it can affect us, and ways we can implement it in our lives.

Chapter One: Guru

I had twenty dollars' worth of quarters in the velvet, drawstring bag, hidden away in my purse. I couldn't make the call from home, or it would show up on my parents' phone bill. I knew intuitively that I shouldn't tell my parents that I would place a phone call to the ashram all the way in India. The phone number to the ashram of the author, Bhagwan Shree Rajneesh (later to be known as Osho), was written in the back of the book. I don't know what I wanted to say to the guru, Rajneesh. I was pulled along by an intense curiosity. I made my way into one of the phone booths in the Student Union Building at UNM, just around the corner from the cafeteria, shut the door, and started to put my coins into the phone – five dollars' worth of quarters for the first minute. The call was placed and I heard the phone ringing at the other end of the line in India. It rang a few times and suddenly it picked up. I heard a voice start to talk. It was the answering machine. I had forgotten about the time difference. It was about three in the morning in India when I called. My initial attempt to reach a guru proved fruitless. I took all my extra quarters and went home.

A guru is a special kind of spiritual teacher who takes the place of the deity for the student, similar to how the deity played the role of the guru for the rishis, over 10,000 years ago: Lord Shiva was the original guru, and he taught first to his wife Parvati, who then taught to the rishis, so they could transmit the knowledge to humanity. The rishis were wise seers who meditated deeply.

While traditionally the term guru refers to a Hindu or tantric spiritual teacher, we have all sorts of gurus or teachers in our lives, and there are many ways we can experience the idea of the guru.

At root, the guru represents the idea of the eternal, divine, teacher. This is not a person but the Divine One who is the invisible teacher, behind the veil of our everyday experience.

Outwardly, all sorts of things in the world can be the guru to us. An ant can be the guru if you are learning something from observing it in the world. Our parents are our first gurus, and our teachers are our gurus, too. For me, in hindsight, therapists have been gurus of their own sort, as I have often sought them out to help me find my way, and connect with my inner wisdom, which is another expression of the guru, called the guru within, or gurave. Even a book can be a guru. If you are a Christian, Jesus is your guru. If you are a wise parent, the child is your guru.

We are here to learn and the guru is eternal. The guru is everywhere, speaking to us through those moments when moving through life we find ourselves learning. The guru is there.

After my initial attempt, I never tried to call the guru Rajneesh again. I forgot about India and the guru for a while after that. I was in college and became busy with the project of moving out of my parents' house. I rented a room at Luther House, an ELCA Lutheran Student Center on campus at UNM. It was affordable, and I was able to pay the rent with a part time job.

I enjoyed living on the university grounds, and loved to visit the interesting book stores around campus. I read up on topics like Wicca from authors like Starhawk, who were classics in their time. I also read a book about Sophia, the Christian Goddess in the Bible. The Sophia movement was a bit of a feminist spirituality movement within the Christian church in the last century.

I got married and my interests in spirituality continued. Learning in books inspired me and I connected with the inner guru – my own innate intelligence. I designed my own spiritual mandala, formed of two intersecting triangles, not a totally unique concept, but little did I know. My main concern was that I was able to have a four pointed system which consisted of Mother God and Father God at the top two corners, and Jesus and Sophia at the bottom two corners.

My husband and I had a daughter and moved with her into our own little house. I know that over the years, I have learned a lot from my daughter and spouse. We learn a lot in relationships, and every time we are learning, the illusive, timeless, divine guru is there.

I became interested in shamanism as I was finishing out my Master's Degree in Creative Writing. I'd say that within shamanism, the dreamtime, or imaginal realm, and spirit helpers are differing expressions of the concept of the guru within and without. Shaman journey by going within into the imaginal realm to learn from teachers within, and also connect with animal helpers in the physical world.

For several years I explored alternative spirituality communities in Yahoo Groups, which were very active at that time. Again, listening to the guru within me, I followed my own impulses and created a couple of my own groups on Yahoo, mostly focused on divine feminine themes. I explored shamanism in groups and even consulted a shaman and got soul retrieval work done. Soul retrieval work is another sort of spiritual tool we can use to integrate the self and making ourselves healed and whole is part of our journey through life. Whenever we are doing work on ourselves and become more self-aware, we are strengthening the inner guru.

Thank God that throughout those early years, before I met Shajesh, I always knew to go within to rejuvenate – to find a dark room, rest in quiet, to listen in, to be with my breath-wave, to meditate, to listen to the guru within. In Tantra, kundalini is also often seen as a guru or a guide within us. And even before kundalini activation we have also the guru in the heart. There is even a tantric practice that involves writing down things from the unconscious to bring them into the conscious, which amounts to the same thing as journaling. All these practices help us to cultivate our connection with our inner guru.

Back online, I found the Indian gurus HRM and Sunyogi Umasankar in western discussion group. I dabbled for a few years in sungazing,

Last but not least, I explored the pranayama practice of a popular Indian guru for a number of years, before finally becoming a yoga teacher. My experience of the guru in that context was remote – the guru was like a far off celebrity, and we did the pranayama while listening to a tape, guided along by the voice of the guru.

Then, rather unexpectedly, when the idea of the guru was farthest from my mind and I was absorbed with the business of being a yoga teacher, thirty three-years after my attempt to call the Rajneesh ashram in India, I met Shajesh in an online yoga group. He has been my real, tantric guru ever since.

Shajesh is a guru in the ancient, tantric, Aananda Nath tradition, a tradition that goes all the way back to the days of Lord Shiva, over 10,000 years ago. Yes, he is my guru, and he has given me his Guru Mantra which can't be shared. In this book, I will be sharing what Shajesh has authorized me to share of these tantric lineage practices. Also, I will share from my personal experience and research.

There are many tantric traditions. I am sharing an introduction to the system I have been trained in.

The guru is very important in Tantra. On p. 53 in *The Tantra of Sri Chakra*, by Prof. S. K. Ramachandra Rao, we find the author quoting the Parananda Sutra which states, enigmatically, in reference to "the master," which is another way of saying "the guru":

> "One must contemplate on the idea that the master is higher than everything; that the sacred word is higher than the master; that the deity is higher than the sacred word; and that one's own transcendental self is higher than the deity."

If I had to replace Shajesh, I would not know where to begin. This has started rather simply and if for some reason I woke up tomorrow and something happened to Shajesh, I don't know what I would do. I'd have to just keep practicing all the practices that I know that I already learned. This beautiful Tantric Japa Yoga story has been unfolding, and I always thought it was beautiful and wanted to know the next phase. If it were to stop unfolding, I would have so many other mantras and practices at my disposal that are mine because my guru gave them to me.

If Shajesh were suddenly gone, I would not, however, know how to go forward in these ancient tantric lineage practices. He has so much more to teach me. And I have learned something about where the studies will go after I complete the current study I am on. I know there is more, and I would not know how to practice it on my own. I'm not saying this out of some sort of servility, or a feeling of false dependency on my guru. Shajesh gives me the assignments, and I do them.

Studies that are more advanced are usually longer and take more than one phase of practice to learn. It is the guru who decides what assignment I get next and how to pace my practice. They are divided up into segments by the guru so that they are learned a little at a time, practicing 45 days for each segment. It took me a whole year to learn Sri Vidya. It would be unreasonable to expect the average person to just suddenly wake up and start practicing such a long practice. Some of the practices are long, such as the tarpanams. But even when there have been multiple practice sessions combined in one day, I think the most I have ever spent practicing is an hour and a half a day. Currently my practice is taking me 35 minutes a day, which is just about right for me now.

Remote Energy

It's very convenient for me that I can meet Shajesh online on Zoom and I do so regularly. It works out very well for me that I don't have to travel to India to be a student of Shajesh. Traveling is hard for me because I had extensive clotting in my left leg when I was a in my twenties, and have had issues with circulation ever since.

They've done studies that show people can track others' feelings through body language over the internet so it's very much like being in the same room with a person. I have been studying from the comfort and ease of my home, taking every accommodation for myself. Not only have I been practicing from the comfort of my own home, meeting with my guru online, but I have all the same lifestyle of the average westerner.

One of the siddhis (special powers) that a guru has is to send energy remotely. Even reiki practitioners do this and I was in an online workshop with a spiritualist who was teaching people how to send each other energy through Zoom. So, this knowledge should help you overcome any inhibition you have to meeting with a tantric guru online. Just know that even by the laws of quantum physics, you will have a meaningful meeting and your energies too can meet one another.

Chapter Two: Sadhana

The word "God" is an English word, but the concept of God as an Absolute Being and the infinite light of consciousness is part of Hinduism as well as Tantra. In fact the concept of God in Hinduism and in Tantra is much older than Christianity. In the West, we tend to associate Christian meaning to the word God, but it is simply the English word for a concept which in Hinduism predates Christianity itself and even predates the English language by several thousand years. Tantra takes its concept of God from the Vedas and Hinduism, not from Christianity or the English Language. Christianity itself emerged in a world that had many gods and the concept of God is not original to Christianity. Hindu and Tantric authors also use the word God at times, when writing in and translating into English.

In Hinduism and Tantra, when we think of God, two things come to mind: *sadhana* or *disciplined spiritual practice* for the purpose of attaining moksha or spiritual liberation; and, *morality* or ideas about how to be a good person, which often means in the eyes of God, or as measured by the idea of certain held values, beautiful ideals, virtues and beliefs about the difference between good and bad. It is believed that when we have good behavior and values, that this progresses us on the path toward moksha. Likewise it is believed that when we do sadhana – disciplined, spiritual practices – that this progresses us on the path toward moksha. The concepts of dharma, yamas and niyamas, and sadhana, are all related to the desire to act in ways that will lead us to moksha or liberation.

Now we will explore and bring together four concepts which are core principles in Hinduism and Tantra: dharma, yamas, niyamas, and sadhana.

These are four concepts which are important to know in relation to our chanting practices, which is called sadhana. Sadhana is a practice that we do. We discipline ourselves to do it. It is a tool for the attainment of the ultimate goal of Tantra, which is the union of Shiva and Shakti in the crown. However, our sadhana will lose meaning and power if we do not live a moral and ethical life, and mindfully pursue dharma. According to Tantra we don't have to give up our activities in the world and may also, in alignment with dharma, pursue artha, kama and moksha. We should also live according to the yamas and niyamas.

Let's consider the four goals of life in Hinduism and Tantra, namely:

1. **Dharma** – right living
2. **Artha** – material sustenance and success
3. **Kama** – successful relationships and love
4. **Moksha** – spiritual liberation or consciousness expansion

The Yamas and Niyamas come from Patanjali's eight limbs of yoga which are:

1. **Yama** – moral discipline, about how to act in the world and towards others
2. **Niyama** – right action with regards to self-management;
3. **Asana** – the physical postures of yoga
4. **Pranayama** – breathing exercises

5. **Pratyahara** – withdrawal of the senses (from sense objects in our objective field of reality, into the inner; world of intuition, consciousness, bliss, meditation)
6. **Dharana** – concentration (such as on specific chakra, point, or image)
7. **Dhyana** – contemplation, which is not the same as discursive thinking. In contemplation the mind is carried along as in a dream or a reverie on a specific topic. Contemplation can be compared to a dance where there is no beginning, no end and no goal, except the dance itself; discursive thinking is goal oriented;
8. **Samadhi** – peace, enlightenment, bliss (resulting from cessation of the discursive mind)

The eight limbs of yoga are a guide for spiritual growth and living a balanced life.

The first two limbs are Yama and Niyama.

Yamas are:

1. **Ahimsa** – non violence
2. **Satya** – truthfulness
3. **Asteya** – not stealing
4. **Brahmacharya** – celibacy or right use of energy
5. **Aparigraha** – non-greed or not hoarding

Niyamas are:

1. **Saucha** – cleanliness
2. **Santosha** – contentment (being happy with what one has)
3. **Tapas** – discipline, austerity, or strong motive
4. **Svadhyaya** – study of self and of sacred texts
5. **Isvara Pranidhana** – surrender to or contemplation of a higher power or God

Now let's consider the word Sadhana:

In Hinduism and in Tantra, sadhana refers to spiritual practices, the goal of which is to achieve spiritual realization, enlightenment, or moksha (liberation from the cycle of death and rebirth). Beyond specific practices, sadhana can also be seen as having a worshipful attitude about everything we do in life: the way we breathe and move and do our daily chores. It is said we should offer all our activity up to the Divine -- to God. If you don't believe in God, or belief in God makes you feel uncomfortable, you can offer your activities up to your higher self, or the higher mind, realizing the mind is consciousness and has the capacity to expand, and acknowledging that creation is bigger than us, and that it holds us in being, not visa-versa. Consciousness, if not the Divine Being or God, is at least a powerful and cosmic force in the universe of which we partake. There is nothing religious about the term cosmic. Cosmic simply means of or relating to the cosmos, the extraterrestrial vastness or the universe. A cosmos is simply a universe. Nothing mysterious there. What we exhale, trees and plants inhale; and we inhale what plants and trees are exhaling. We are part of a larger web of life, which sustains us.

Specific practices that may be considered Sadhana are:

1. **Meditation** – practices which focus the mind in such a way as to invite relaxed alertness, to quiet the mind in order to achieve samadhi
2. **Pranayama** – conscious breathing exercises
3. **Svadyaya** – self-study and/or study of sacred scripture
4. **Visualization** – consciously creating a desired image through the trained imagination
5. **Dhyana** – contemplation

6. **Dharana** – concentration as on a specific point or image
7. **Self-discipline** – anything we have to do such as work, family responsibilities, daily chores, and going to school, etc
8. **Asana** – practicing physical postures of yoga helps keep prana flowing in the body and through the chakras, which is part of spiritual development. Even modern science is now telling us that based on research, physical activity is good for the mind and emotions
9. **Mantra Japa** – chanting Sanskrit mantras creates special effects in us that are not achieved by other methods, and which aid in activating prana and waking up kundalini
10. **Prarthana** – prayer: the most popular form of prayer in Hinduism is to chant mantras while evoking the deity through feelings of the heart (prayer of the heart). You can bring the hands into anjali mudra (prayer posture) in front of the heart and say a direct prayer to the deity about what you are chanting for before you begin, which is also called setting an intention.

When we are doing sadhana, we don't have to do all the types listed. The list gives some options we have to choose from when creating our personal sadhana.

If we analyze these concepts of dharma, yama, niyama, and sadhana, we can see that they are all woven together. Some aspects of sadhana are also included in the eight limbs of yoga.

One main take away that we should get from this is how important reverence is. When we do all our acts with a sense of reverence for the divine, or for the higher expressions of consciousness, or the web of life, or whatever it is that we identify with a "higher power," this is the attitude of sadhana that we take into our daily activities. When out of a sense of reverence, we take up meditation in hopes of evolving our souls and our consciousness, this too is sadhana or a form of disciplined activity toward the end goal of yoga.

Really, having an attitude of sadhana is just a way of saying that we are living our lives with respect and offering all our actions up to a higher power or principle. It means we want to live a balanced life and to evolve ethically and consciously as people. Having an attitude of sadhana is, in a way, like caring about living our dharma. Even while we are earning a living, we can let all our actions come from a place of detachment, without attachment to an end result, offering all we do up to a higher power or value.

If we are unethical in how we are making a living, we aren't living according to dharma and it's not ok. If we are unethical about how we earn a living, we will be unethical in our soul, and how can we build healthy, good relationships and love, on top of unethical attitudes and behavior? Dharma comes first because living according to dharma is what gives integrity to the other three goals in life. Moksha too is dependent on dharma. If we can't live ethically, according to dharma, what difference will it make if we meditate, since our behavior will be holding us back and our meditations will be unfruitful, as they are being done on the foundation of a divided self? How can we be one with the source when we are stuck in unethical living and our left hand doesn't even know what our right hand is doing? If we are deceiving others, we are deceiving ourselves that it is ok to live out of alignment with cosmic law. Cosmic law wants us to be good.

Or you could say that God wants us to be good and so we have these laws to remind ourselves.

Belief in God is not necessary. Atheists can take up sadhana and pursue moksha as a state of expanded consciousness. But one still has to have a moral code, and reverence for something, like a concept of a higher organizing principal, like the web of life, or humanity, or the cosmos, or cosmic consciousness – whatever you can define that captures the idea of a higher power or value to you, so that you have something to reach for, some greater reality to feel humbled before.

Why Meditate Regularly?

Meditation is sadhana and is one of the things we can do to help ourselves deal with life. Meditation supports our personal growth, and we should strive to make meditation a regular part of our lives.

In Tantric Japa Yoga, it is important to meditate regularly because the effects of the practices are cumulative over time. We are to continue learning and striving to evolve over many lifetimes until we succeed at achieving moksha – or union of Shiva and Shakti in the crown. And even before we achieve that, we meditate to keep ourselves going in the right direction and to give ourselves every support, by strengthening our connection to the inner world.

If you are a person for whom meditation can solve problems immediately, and you meditate one time and all your baggage drops away from you, and you become a new person, and you no longer have any issues, that would be a big surprise. It would be just as big of a surprise as if you walked into the gym and had never worked out a day in your life, and after picking up a ten pound hand weight you expect to be able to go lift a 200 pound barbell. Or you go to the cardio machine, or the treadmill, or the bike, and exert yourself a little, and you feel great afterward, maybe you feel a little fitter and the waist of your pants feels a little looser. But you have to keep doing that over and over and over at the gym for one year, then two years. You can't just work out one time and expect transformation in your body, and your mind is no different. You will have to meditate over and over and over again, many times, and over time you will make changes. Sure you will feel better after meditating and you can practice samadhi after you do pranayama and chant, and with time, and repeat effort, you will slowly get better at it. You will slowly make changes.

And just like you can't quit working out at the gym after you've made a year or two of changes to your body. You have to still keep with it to maintain your fitness level and to have a healthy lifestyle. Meditation is no different.

I'd like to encourage everyone to continue to meditate their whole life long, because it helped me persevere. It helped me keep my center. I started to do chanting and it helped me, and still I needed therapy even though I was meditating and I kept meditating. I began to doubt myself, thinking I wasn't good enough because I still needed therapy, but after a few years of therapy my meditation improved and I started to experience kundalini.

You can even go to the psychiatrist if need be, and they will give you a pill and you can take one, if you like, and keep meditating. You don't have to be without problems or struggles to meditate and get benefits. The Divine One can negotiate all your life experiences, can see when you are making your best effort, and meets you where you are. If something helps you to be a stronger container – if something helps you hold your own center – that will help you find the space mentally and emotionally for meditation in your life.

But if meditation is not bringing you peace, don't do it. Take a break for a while and refocus yourself.

Reverence

I just met with Shajesh today. He seems so alive with energy to me. When he moves his arms this way or that, to me he seems like a being of light. He's been studying and practicing for 35 years and I have been studying and practicing for just over ten.

And I just assume and think it is safe to say that the extent of his knowledge reaches far beyond mine, and this is in part because he has been on the path much longer than me, and in part because he is from the culture of origin of Tantra. From birth, he was steeped in and surrounded by Hindu and Tantric cultures. If there were religious festivals he was there. If people were chanting on the river, he was there – everything he has been absorbing from childhood until now, beyond the years spent actually studying in this ancient tantric lineage.

I think one of the things that Shajesh has been more steeped in than I have been as a westerner, is the sense of awe and reverence. This is something we need to cultivate. We can get a mantra here and a mantra there and we are at liberty to chant whatever we want – whatever we find on the internet – but there is no rhyme or reason to it.

The characters and themes of mantras and nyasas in TJY are part of a whole cosmology, rich in meaning, as the practices unfold before us. It's not just individual deities that are important, but how they fit into the bigger picture and we

27

learn to have a sense of perspective for the meaning and majesty of the tantric spirituality, rather than remaining isolated to one fragment of the big picture. This broader comprehension of the overall meaning, helps us to see the value in our practices and valuing something is the foundation of reverence.

Tantra is steeped in a sense of awe and reverence. The creation is real on one level. But on another level it's an illusion because there is more to it than meets the eye and what it is really made of is hidden, a mystery, cloaked in atoms and electrons and protons and quantum qualities. It veils our essential nature and keeps us preoccupied with externals, with the objective world. But Tantra has this refined sense of inner realities, otherwise referred to as subjective reality. And this subjective reality, which is inner reality, is mysterious and illusive, veiled in feelings and sensations and the experience of consciousness, energy and being.

There is this sense of awe and wonder about the inner world. This awe and wonder about the inner world leads to a healthy sense of reverence. Reverence is a form of respect that recognizes the deep abiding value of something.

In the West, we want to analyze and dissect everything objectively. And we do it with a sense of scientific precision that seems a little cool. It's all very intellectual. There is analysis in tantric philosophy as well. However, much of the analysis is of subtle energy realms, or subjective experience, which is all treated as if it is real.

Respecting Our Inner Experience: Realizing Similarities between Tantric and Other Forms of Practice.

Regarding the nature of the reality of our subjective inner experience, I have found that there is some overlap in understanding between one modality of psychology and certain tools of Tantra. "Inner-child work," which I learned from my most recent therapist who I have worked with for several years now, uses certain tools which can be used to illustrate certain aspects of Tantra, and I will try to explain this.

In inner-child work, we imagine our inner-child. Then we also imagine an ideal, loving parent. Then in the inner world of our imagination, through journaling, we have these two parts interact. This is a construct that is created through the use of our imagination and has its own reality. We know it has reality because we can interact with it and this brings profound changes in emotion and improves our ability to cope.

Meanwhile, in Tantra we have the nirguna or formless aspect of the deity which we cannot fathom, and is beyond our capacity to imagine. Then on the other hand we have the saguna aspect of the deity who has a visual form, such as Lord Shiva. We create the visual image of Lord Shiva with our imagination, much like we create the image of the wise inner parent and the inner-child in inner-child work. But there is a sort of reality to our imagination, which we can pray to and interact with, and we can chant Om Namah Shivaya and vibrate on the same wavelength as Lord Shiva. And the mantra creates a real vibration, a real sound that has reality, and chanting this creates physical effects in our body and mind, such as perhaps most notably, relaxation, which is real. In fact, the mantras are all constructed not randomly, but consciously by combining the sacred sounds of the Matrika, the letters of the Sanskrit alphabet, to create certain effects in the energy body and the mind.

We don't have to understand the whole science of Matrika to have an intuitive sense of this idea. The sounds of the mantras have specific effects on us that are real. All we have to do is chant the mantras, and through practice, we can observe our experience of the various mantras and observe that they each have their own energy and their own effects. The same is true of music and songs: different melodies clearly produce different effects in us. These are real effects created by the real use of sound in songs and in mantra.

So chanting mantras and experiencing the vibrations, as well as visualizing the deity and developing a rapport inwardly with the deity all have their own level of reality.

Even thoughts by themselves are subtle vibrations created in the brain by movement through the brain, which is why people who do dhyana meditation can also activate kundalini. Focusing the mind on visual images and meanings in a flow as is done in dhyana meditation or contemplation, surely creates some energy flow. With chanting out loud there is that added element of the physical vibration of the actual sound.

The thing is: our inner experiences come from the Divine Mother. This is a Goddess working her magic in us. Shakti is also Maya, the Goddess who veils the ultimate reality so we can experience individuality and diversity, including our inner experience. Our inner reality is to be approached with the greatest reverence. It is a manifestation of divine intelligence. It is not just a topic to devour in a book and then set aside.

We think the universe is inert matter, that we, the conscious human beings, act upon. Indeed, consciousness reaches its highest expression in the animal kingdom with humans. And as the highest expression of consciousness in the animal kingdom, we also have the capacity for spiritual, mystical, metaphysical, and emotional experience.

Yet, one is not supposed to rely on experiences to keep one meditating any more in Tantra than one is supposed to rely on miracles to keep one praying in the Bible. One meditates to give one's soul support in the process of evolving over time. When kundalini starts to become more active, and if you start to feel it, that will be great. But we have to have reverence. Reverence is the most important thing. And we can have the grace to let go of spiritual experience and go about our daily lives, as this leaves the way open to the unexpected. If we have preconceived notions, we are trying too hard to steer the experience, which may unfold in ways we don't otherwise expect. Spiritual experiences are artifacts of our spiritual unfolding. Enjoy them when they occur and know they point to something more.

The meditation process is so that the meditator will evolve spiritually and develop spiritual abilities, such as enhanced intuition and inner sight: some see auras or have a more active third-eye, and above all, experiencing expanded states of consciousness. Now, the expanded state of consciousness is also considered a state of bliss, and it's also considered a state of kundalini awakening. It's the fact that kundalini causes us to expand our awareness and in that context we may begin to experience things in a new way.

Shajesh explained to me that in Tantra, when the sperm and the egg unite in the womb, there is an egg head with a tail on it. In the egg part is the crown chakra with 1,000 petals, and in the tail part there are all six remaining chakras. Then as the body of the baby develops, the physical body grows out of the chakras. We literally emerge as physical manifestations out of this energetic programming that at a spiritual level is the source of the actual physical creation. We emerge out of spiritual reality, and as we experience expanded states of consciousness, we start to have more respect for inner, subjective realities.

Chapter Three: Chanting

It was the year 2008 and I was in India, in Mumbai, up at five am in the predawn dark, on the third floor of my hotel where I spent the night. I stood, looking out over the city, in front of the big picture window in my room. I saw rickshaws, and cars, and people walking, down on the busy street. The sounds of tooting and driving drifted up through the air. As I stood there, other sounds began to enter my awareness: the *Sounds of Chanting*. One or more persons were chanting out loud in the hotel. Early morning hours are believed to be good for chanting and other forms of meditation as well.

One of the tools that Tantra uses to achieve liberation is chanting. Chanting is one of the ways we can begin to still the discursive mind, and refresh the energy in the body. Since liberation involves achieving a still mind that has experienced the ground of its own being, japa is a tool of Tantra for the purpose of moksha. Moksha means liberation and in Tantra, moksha entails the union of Shiva and Shakti in the crown, often referred to as kundalini awakening.

Tantric Japa Yoga is all about chanting in Sanskrit in order to raise one's vibration, evolve, and connect with divinity. Japa is the repetition of a mantra. Tantra means to weave together. Yoga means to yoke together. What is woven, yoked and connected is the spiritual and the physical. The tool that is being used to achieve the purpose of weaving together and yoking, is japa. Tantric Japa Yoga also weaves together bhukti and mukti, or the life of a householder, and the life of a spiritual seeker, all within a single individual. One doesn't have to run off and become a wandering sadhu (ascetic), though one certainly can, and the wandering sadhus have their own social and spiritual status. In Tantra, one can be a householder and still be involved with ones worldly life, and can achieve moksha or liberation at the same time. One doesn't have to go to the ashram and isolate oneself from the world. One can be in the world, and weave spirituality into one's daily life, yoking one's goals and intents to the divine. One can become jivamukti, or liberated while living, which amounts to achieving expanded consciousness and oneness with God as a result of Shiva and Shakti uniting in the crown – otherwise known as kundalini awakening.

One of the reasons that chanting is a tool of Tantra is that Tantra is all about the spiritual vibrations. Mantras vibrate. Mantras vibrate our whole nature on all levels when chanted out loud. According to Tantra, when chanted out loud, mantras purify the air and all our surroundings, as well as our own body and all our five elements that we are made of (earth, water, fire, air, and ether). Scientific research shows that mantra chanting also stimulates cerebral spinal fluid flow and the vagus nerve, and does other things, like reducing cortisol in the brain. Chanting mantras out loud is beautiful and beneficial. Chanting out loud does not entail a melody in the full sense of the word, though there may be some subtle melodic tones to it. Chanting is not musical, though bhajan and kirtan are musical ways to approach chanting in which the mantras are sung along to music with instruments in a group.

Chanting: Out Loud

Chanting can be done out loud. In India much chanting is done rather loudly. Priests chant along the Ganges for all to hear.

The mantra is vibrations. The mantra is words. Words are vibrations when spoken. When spoken out loud words are used between people as tools for communication. We have been given vocal cords for the purpose of speaking, and our spoken words are all vibrations. It's not just mantras that vibrate. Cars honking their horns down on the street are creating vibrations, and the chanters are creating their own vibrations. People go to hear gong and singing bowl for sound bath. Bathing in the sound vibrations has been shown to be relaxing and to have other benefits. Chanting out loud is a sound bath for your ears and your whole body.

The voice of God, otherwise known as Vak Devi, who is the Goddess of Speech, is a very important Shakti in Tantra. Through her cosmic vocalizations she creates the phenomenal world. Her speech is said to include four levels of vocalization. Speaking out loud so others can hear is one of those forms. So to express Goddess Vak in her fullness it is appropriate to make use of all the forms of speech, from silent to quiet to spoken out loud.

Chanting out loud is good. It develops the vocal cords and exercises the breath. I have been chanting out loud in my home in the suburbs for over ten years now. Often I even chant with the windows open or ajar, in spring, summer, autumn, and sometimes even in winter. I go in my home and shut the doors, and am safe and private in my home, but surely my voice drifts. Sometimes I can hear my neighbors talk, though I usually don't, and mostly don't make out what they are saying when I do. I live in a quiet neighborhood on an acre, so there is space between homes, but we still have neighbors close enough to talk over the fence on the one side. There are houses all around me. Two are in earshot across the street, and one on the other side is in earshot if the windows are open. I used to worry about this a little. But Shajesh told me, if anyone hears me they won't know what I am doing, won't know what I am chanting, won't know. And I didn't worry about it much after that. In fact, often I chant rather loudly, even when windows are open in summer.

It's true. If anyone hears me chanting – and I'm confident that in ten years' time, that probably at some time, somebody heard my sounds – they will just hear the sounds as I heard in the hotel in Mumbai, of mantra drifting through the air. They won't know what I am chanting, probably won't give it much thought.

Sure I make some efforts to be private, as I said. I don't go out and chant on my front porch. I don't even go out in my back yard, out on the hill, under the big oak tree, and chant there, where neighbors from all sides could see me and probably even hear my sounds. I enjoy the privacy of my home.

Traditionally, it is appropriate to seek some degree of privacy for chanting, which is a form of meditation. For one thing, you don't want other people's sounds to bother you, and if you hear sounds, it's ok but it's appropriate to try to find a place to meditate where sounds are at least a little bit dulled so they are not distracting.

It's not practical to try to chant or meditate inside a sound proof vault and it's not necessary. It might be a luxury that some may enjoy, to have a whole spare room in your home to devote to meditation; but even that will probably not be sound proof. Even in a home, chanting and other sounds can be heard through closed doors and walls, as I heard it in the hotel in Mumbai. And as my husband hears me when I do my chanting daily at home.

I have been chanting in the suburbs for over ten years, the song of my soul drifting out into the neighborhood, vivifying the air around me. I might start a little timid; but I don't take long to forget my surroundings and become absorbed in my chanting.

Chanting out loud fills up the head with sound and absorbs our total focus. The head is filled with vibration. The skull literally vibrates. The chest vibrates. The throat and the soft palate in the mouth vibrates, the vocal cords vibrate, and we develop a rich melodious speaking voice. The whole body vibrates. And we exercise our lungs with all the breathing we have to do in order to accomplish all the chanting.

Exercise your freedom and let your song ring out. Even though mantra is not melodic like a song, it is its own sort of song that the soul sings. Let the soul sing out. Can you imagine being given vocal cords by the creator and then told you can't ever open your mouth and use them? Sure, people go to silence retreats. Silence can be a deep spiritual practice that feeds the soul, and a healthy part of all of our lives. Have you heard the silence vibrating after a session of chanting out loud? Silence rushes in, the mind is stilled.

It's not as if the mantra is noise. You have to chant with a good quality tone. You have to *vibrate*. Mantra affects the total vibrations all around you, so make the best and the richest tone possible. Let yourself ring like a bell with the mantra tones as they move through you. Let your entire vehicle be like the singing bowl.

Chanting out loud frees the soul and is a beautiful expression of soulfulness. The louder you chant the easier it will be to focus. It's enjoyable and it should be a regular part of your sadhana.

For one thing, enunciation is important and it's important to know how to say the words correctly – especially for somebody who has not grown up surrounded by Sanskrit sounds. It's important at least at first, to chant out loud, to practice enunciation and be sure you are mastering the actual sounds with your actual vocal cords. Personally, I feel it is important culturally as well, because most of us have not grown up surrounded by Sanskrit sounds, and we are not familiar with the sounds. We should become familiar with Sanskrit sounds by learning to make them with our own voice, learning to overcome the inhibition toward making foreign sounds. For one thing, in Tantra, when we chant out loud, it is believed that the tongue's contact with various places in the mouth creates shifts in energy and consciousness and can take us deeper in meditation.

Chanting is Cosmic Vibrations

Chanting mantra entails predominantly and primarily the making of certain sounds, over and over and over. A mantra is a sacred word or group of words whose sounds are believed to raise energy and consciousness through their vibrations. The sound of the mantra is very sacred. As tantric practitioners, we should pay attention to the vibrations as we chant. It's all about the vibrations. The mantra vibrates through one's system and makes changes in the body. Some of the changes it makes have been scientifically studied.

As a result of vibrations from chanting, we may experience changes in how we feel as we go about our day. We may notice feeling a little bit more detached, or calmer.

We may come to look forward to chanting because of the benefits we feel. Things we have had difficulties with may start to seem like less of a problem or may evaporate completely. This is a sign that the mantra japa is doing what it is supposed to do. Mantra japa helps us to evolve and grow, erasing old samskaras. In Hinduism and in Tantra, samskaras are impressions from the past, like traumas, or other life experiences, that leave programming, complexes and emotional blocks. We have to heal our samskaras, get over the past, and set down new programming. The vibrations created by mantra japa help with this process.

Mantra japa is also one more way of tuning in to our inner realities, and this may be considered a process of spiritual growth. As we focus outward in life, we get things done, and when we focus inward in life, we move closer to our self. The vibrations of the mantra permeate our senses and our body, pulling our attention into our inner realms, our own inner vibration or spanda, the vibration of consciousness – the cosmic vibration of the very soul.

This is what all the yogic practices are about ultimately and all TJY practices as well: they are all about the vibrations helping us to be more in tune with our inner self and with the divine, which we shall learn have more to do with one another than we might at first suspect. The goal being ultimately, that we grow spiritually, and one day reach moksha through a process of spiritual awakening – which is the inner knowledge from experience that we are one with God, the Absolute, the Brahman, or Shiva and Shakti.

There is a lot of esoteric science behind how all the vibrations affect us in very cosmic ways, and a lot of esoteric science behind what the vibrations are. We don't have to understand all the esoteric science in order to enjoy chanting mantras and the effects this brings.

For one thing, it is obvious to us when we make a sound with our vocal device that we are making vibrations. But when we chant silently, where do the vibrations go? Are we still making vibrations when we chant silently? The answer is yes: but they are more subtle vibrations.

In fact, if we imagine back to a time when it is said that the first sound arose in the process of cosmic creation, it first arose out of Lord Shiva, who is consciousness. The primordial sound from which creation springs forth is called nada, and Om is the outward expression – the audible form of nada. We can speculate on the cosmic nature of this first sound because there was no vocal apparatus and there were no ears to hear. The physical creation had not yet happened and God was pure consciousness and energy. We can make the assumption that the consciousness that emitted the sound vibration, as consciousness of the ultimate order, consciousness as God, has the capacity for cosmic hearing and cosmic sound. The original cosmic sound is said to be the Om vibration.

So what do we do when we chant the Om, the simplest of mantras? On one level we just chant. On one level when we chant Om out loud it just *feels* cosmic. The soul sings and it feels very soothing to the soul. Studies have been done on Om chanting and it is actually physically beneficial. One such study was published in the International Journal of Yoga, and is reposted on the National Institutes of Health website. [1] An experiment was done using the audible Om vibration which is noted has the capacity to stimulate the vagus nerve. The Om chanting group was compared to a group who chanted the 'ssss' sound. Those who chanted Om were shown to have reduced activity in the amygdala and in the limbic system. The conclusion is that other studies have shown Om chanting to stimulate the vagus nerve, and all these findings together suggest that chanting Om out loud could have therapeutic value.

Om chanting also stimulates cerebral spinal fluid flow, and reduces cortisol in the brain, all good for us. Just making the sound over and over and over, out loud, is good for us. On the other hand, Om is one mantra you can easily make silently, on the inhale and the exhale, due to its simplicity.

Chanting and the Mind

One thing we can do while chanting the mantra is just simply chant it and become absorbed in the sounds and vibrations: don't worry about the meaning of the mantra. But the mind is very active and while repeating the mantra over and over even silently, the brain will start to think and try to intrude on your meditation; and you can't let yourself think discursively or your attention will be taken away from your chanting; so bring your attention back to your chanting. Also, the heart may put images before your mind's eye (in chidakasha), imbued with feeling and meaning. These images are more like a dream, and dreams are produced in this way while we sleep; these we cannot stop to contemplate

---

[1] The article is entitled: Neurohemodynamic correlates of 'OM' chanting: A pilot functional magnetic resonance imaging study (IntJYoga. 2011 Jan-Jun; 4(1)3-6.doi:10.4103/0973-6131.78171) (PMCID:PMC3099099 PMID:21654968).

while we chant, but we can let them go to God as we chant, like a prayer of the heart, and just let the feelings roll out of us and continue to bring our focus back to our chanting. The mind is vast and complex and the brain is just a vehicle of the mind. In Tantra, the heart is the seat of the mind. Chanting deactivates the limbic system, the part of the brain responsible for stress; it will quiet the discursive mind, and let the feelings flow. Usually, when we are stressed out, our mind is overly active and can't stop thinking, and the feelings do not flow. But when we meditate, the mind is stilled and the feelings begin to flow.

Dhyana

Dhyana is contemplation.

One thing we can do while chanting the mantra is let the mind contemplate the meaning of the mantra itself. On the one hand we don't want to do discursive thinking while chanting. We want to get out of the discursive thinking never ending loop, and let the mind relax. On the other hand, the mind is very active and we don't want to fight with it either, which won't bring good meditation anyway. We just want to continue to bring our focus back to chanting, and focus on the vibration we make, and this will interrupt any potential for discursive thinking that might arise and reduce it to a fleeting emotion or a passing flash of insight. Just keep chanting and contemplate the meaning of the mantra.

To contemplate something is not the same thing as to think about something discursively. Contemplation is more like a dream or a dance. If you contemplate the meaning of the mantra it may take the form of flashes of image that encapsulate what the mantra means or the states it will produce.

The discursive mind does the analytical thinking and problem solving. It is the part of the mind we can't quiet down when worries assail us. The discursive mind chatters on and on and sometimes doesn't like to settle down to sleep. The discursive mind is the one that is referred to as Monkey Mind, because it's all over the place, and is quick to react or become agitated.

Contemplation springs from a mind that has been quieted from discursive thinking. Contemplation has more qualities of image flowing with feeling, like a dream, and can be a refreshing source of healing insight.

Chanting by itself is called japa. But if you are contemplating the meaning of the mantra, that is dhyana or contemplation and it is beneficial to contemplate. For instance, if you are chanting Om, it's ok for impressions of the vastness of Om to arise, how Om is the original vibration, how this whole world is an emanation of the original Om vibration. You can let your imagination be focused on Om while you chant Om. Mostly you just do the chanting and let your mind contemplate on the meaning of Om, instead of letting your mind wander on whatever is stressing you out. So adding dhyana to japa can increase concentration if you are having a hard time turning down the volume in your brain of everything that is stressing you out – all the business of the mind.

Still, you cannot do discursive thinking. If you contemplate Om, while you are chanting Om, the focus still has to be on the chanting and the contemplation may be as it arises, and as it goes. Don't *try* to think about it discursively. Just let impressions about Om come and go, and your feelings go out over your throat on the sound of the mantra.

Let your mind be focused on the mantra, but from your heart, feelings may flow through the mantra and this is ok. The heart is a center of the mind in Tantra, and the heart produces these flashes of image that are imbued with feeling and resemble a dream, or a prayer of the heart.

Inner Experiences

Some individuals may have inner experiences from chanting or other forms of meditation and peoples' experiences will differ, so you won't know what to expect. Then if you expect something and it doesn't happen, you may feel disappointed. On the other hand, if no mention is made of any experience or the possibility of one, a person may not know how to react if experiences do arise, or may lack hope for what is possible. In truth, the inner self is what yoga is all about.

Mantra chanting is having its effect even when we don't have any experiences. This is where faith comes in and the belief that your practice will bring some benefit into your life. And, you probably won't have to wait long for some sort of experience, even if the first experience you have is not of kundalini or the subtle energy of the mantra, but of something else. For instance you might notice a shift in your mind after doing your practices, and subtle or profound changes in how you feel. You may feel tingling in your chakras sometimes in the third-eye between the brows. While chanting, one might notice the vibration in one part of the body and then in another at times, and at other times it might seem as if the vibrations vanish into thin air. Sometimes we might even feel irritation, sitting down to practice, wondering if we are wasting our time, being eccentric, chanting Sanskrit words, that we have a hard time pronouncing.

Purpose of Chanting

The purpose of chanting is to vibrate on the same wavelength with the divine, and often with specific deities and their vibrations, thereby becoming one with deity – one with the Divine One.

God is not there like a vending machine to pop out our desires when we put in a few coins or a little bit of effort or petition. God is all about wanting us to evolve spiritually and to discover our inner self. To that end, the chanting, the vibrations, do slowly over time, neutralize negative content in the brain, and wash trauma and stress out of the body. The process of meditating with chanting, and working with the inner vibrations, is a purifying process that cleans the old samskaras, which are impressions programmed into us through past experiences, difficulties and trauma. After the samskara is purified, a new, healthy one is laid down.

When I first began my chanting practices over ten years ago. I chanted the simplest mantra, but I felt the effects right away – felt that calm, that composure come over me, felt that lift after chanting. It helped me with some difficulties, and it kept me progressing on the path. Life happens, and sometimes situations get to us, make us sad, stressed or traumatized, and sometimes things affect us very deeply and healing takes time. We are going through this life exposed, and maybe like Ganesh with his one tusk, we will have to break something off to get some other job done. But we keep moving forward.

I remember how in my eighth year of TJY practice I was going through some emotional upheaval, coming out of the pandemic, I was in therapy, and I was having a heavy time. For almost a whole year I didn't chant. Then I started to chant again one day, and right away I started to have subtle energy experiences from the chanting. I started to experience kundalini energy. I wasn't expecting it, and nobody could have described it. Some things we just don't know until we go through it ourselves. The experiences I had definitely were something new. I had a profound shift in my experience. I've felt energy all the time when meditating after that. It has been two about two years and I'm still exploring the energy. It's made my practice more noticeably and profoundly transformative and enjoyable – things I worked on for years in therapy, falling away with no effort, being soothed by the subtle vibrations of the chanting in my chakras and my energy field. It's so nice.

One way or another the mantra will affect us – when we notice it affecting us, and when we don't notice it. We are all evolving for lifetimes and everyone is different. Somebody else might start to feel the subtle energy sooner than I did and yet, I had a few metaphysical experiences way back in college years before I ever had any formal training in meditative practices. On one level it's just a part of who we are. People in various traditions all over the world have had energy, spiritual, and metaphysical experiences. Chanting japa is one way to carry the soul along in paths where such things may happen.

Chanting Practice: Consistency and Other Factors

If you are chanting, it's best to have a daily practice. Try to be consistent and regular with your practice. Make a formal time each day to meditate.

In the practices that I did for my guru, I had a forty five day practice period for each phase. I would like to say based on this, that if you take up a new mantra and are chanting it independently of a guru, you should chant it formally each day for a specific time, regularly, for forty five days, out loud. Then, in between your daily practice sessions, you can do what you want. Just start chanting the mantra you've learned, any time – like you would sing in the shower or sing while cleaning your kitchen, instead you may chant. And if you take up TJY practice, over time it will give you mantras that are yours to chant, given to you by your guru.

Make a regular time each day as your daily practice time, and in that time, formally chant the mantra out loud. Get familiar with its vibrations. In forty five days of formal practice, you are making the mantra yours; in forty five days of practice, there is a whole process of purification going on that takes forty five days to complete; also about forty five days is how long one does a new practice before it starts to become a habit. Then if you want to chant the mantra in addition to your regular practice, feel free. Chant it out loud, or very quietly, or silently if you wish, in your free time. But do not shirk your duty and your privilege to liberate the Sanskrit sounds from your throat, your mouth, your vocal cords, and your voice, to liberate yourself from inhibition, and to become familiar with the Sanskrit vibrations.

You can chant out loud while washing the dishes or folding the laundry. You can chant quietly under your breath while taking another load of laundry to the washing machine and you can chant silently in your mind while taking the other load out of the dryer. You can chant like this as you are able throughout the day. If you don't feel like doing housework or some other chore, chanting can help you get moving and can carry you through the task. Chanting raises the energy in the body and is refreshing to the system. Chanting gives the Monkey Mind less opportunity to distract itself. You can chant for a while out loud, or quietly, or silently to yourself, from one to another, as is appropriate for your situation, as you move through your day, falling silent when your day takes too much of your focus to continue with chanting.

Sometimes the mind just falls silent and we find ourselves beyond the discursive mind, absorbed with some task at hand, enjoying the silence.

And if your day is taking so much from you that you can't chant as you go, you can find a quiet place and take five minutes or even a minute or two, and chant, out loud if you can, quietly, or silently. If you are stressed out it will feel very nice to expel some breath and make the sound over your vocal cords and your throat. And if you chant it silently, let your breath move in sync with your silent rhythm, exhaling as you mentally chant Om, and inhaling in the pause, or making another om silently with the inhale.

There are all sorts of situations one might chant in: cleaning the kitchen, folding the laundry, and even washing your hair. While you are vacuuming and shampooing your carpets you can chant Lakshmi Mantra if you like, because Goddess Lakshmi likes cleanliness and orderliness, and she likes it when we keep our affairs in order. So go ahead and chant Lakshmi Mantra while you bath or clean or beautify yourself, or while you cook, or set the table for your guests.

Or if, like I am today, you are having a little bit of a sad day and you just feel the overwhelming speechlessness of it all, you can chant Om or Om Namah Shivaya.

You can chant while you are worried about a problem – you can chant a Ganesh Mantra to remove obstacles. You can chant Om Namah Shivaya and meditate on the vastness of consciousness and how consciousness could solve your problem, and visualize Lord Shiva covered in white ash with the Ganges flowing through his wild hair, meditating, and maybe the answer will come to you while you chant, as your concern goes out like a prayer from your heart on your soul's vibration as you chant your mantra.

One way or another, you will be adding minutes, and even hours to your practice, and if you are keen to activate or awaken kundalini, in this way you may hasten yourself along the path. And if you don't want to do extra chanting, you don't have to: just do your formal practice regularly each day, for however long you are assigned; and when kundalini starts to wake up you may want to chant the mantras more, at least sometimes, because of the beautiful feelings they bring inside. Of course, you may find yourself enjoying the silence as well.

When we are chanting the mantra out loud, it's easy to feel the vibration, and even still, we are not used to using our attention in that way to listen in to our bodies and feel vibration, but it happens all the time when we are simply talking. Talking creates vibrations in the head and the body. The thing about mantras, is that sound is used in mantras in a more conscious and deliberate way to create specific vibration experiences in the body. For instance, if you are chanting Om, the o vibrates more in the chest and the m vibrates more in the top of the head. You can make an experiment to verify the truth of this claim. This is not purely esoteric or metaphysical. Sound is vibrations and when we make the vibrations with our own vocal apparatus it travels through our head, and really through our whole body, as it emits out into space.

Exercise

Hold one hand on your heart and one hand on top of your head and chant Om a few times until you can feel the vibration in your hands. You will need to make a good vibration, so you can practice that. Make a nice, resonating vibration and strong sound. Let the energy of Om go out and purify the space around you, as it purifies your own body and mind on its way out.

Now, with one hand on your heart and one hand on your head, make a few Oooom with a long oooo and feel where the vibration is the strongest; then, make a few Ommmm with a long m, and feel where the vibration is the strongest.

Vak Devi and Levels of Speech

Silent chanting is very good, especially once one can experience it more, thanks to kundalini. And chanting out loud is also very nice. They are all good (quiet, silent and out loud) ways to chant, and all are necessary to express the full range of Vak Devi, Goddess of speech, who expresses four levels of the word, namely: the silent (that exists just in the mind); the very quiet like a whisper; fully out loud; and last but not least, transcendental speech, which is beyond our concept of what words are and speech is. And each of the levels of speech are said to contain the other three in some measure. But to make the spoken word, grounds it down into the most basic form of speech, and in some way makes the process of sounding the word complete. This is an esoteric science and books are written just about Vak and how she creates the creation with her transcendental word. Suffice to say, I have heard that making the utterance ourselves out loud completes the circuit – expresses the complete range of various forms of speech, grounding it into our physical realm.

We live in the physical realm. If we want to be jivamukti, or liberated while we live in this life, we still need to take care of our bodies. Ayurveda is the branch of Hinduism that is concerned with our bodily well-being: both physical and mental. Ayurveda also prescribes practices such as pranayama and japa because they are each good for us as spirits living in a body.

Bhukti is all that is for enjoyment in this life, and mukti is all that is for liberation of the soul. According to Tantra we can have both: bhukti and mukti. We can be jivamukti or have liberation of the soul while we still live in and enjoy this life. And that includes enjoying the vibrations and sounds we can make when chanting out loud, as well as enjoying any spiritual experience we may have as part of our spiritual growth. There are actual physical benefits of chanting out loud and letting the sound roll over our vocal cords. Chanting out loud grounds the vibrations down into the body.

Can you imagine if somebody told you, it's good to sing, and singing is good for you, but silent song is the best: just singing silently in your head is best, is the highest form of the song? And who hasn't woken up in the morning to find the lines of some song one heard the day before, going over and over like a mantra through your head silently? The soul loves to sing and enjoys all the vibrations it makes out into space with its vocal apparatus. The soul enjoys using the vehicle of the body to sing. We are to practice ahimsa or non-violence to our body. Singing brings joy and joy brings relaxation and peace and that is all soothing and good for the body. So why stop singing? Out loud, luxuriating in the rich, vibrant tone. Chanting mantras can be like this when you begin to love it and your soul loves the sacred sounds it can make with its vocal apparatus and the experience of feeling the vibrations in the body, an energy bath for the body and for one's surroundings. And, you may wake up some morning with the mantra going silently through your mind like a song. Beautiful physical benefits come from chanting out loud. Let your soul sing. It's good for your soul and it's good for your body.

Subtle Vibrations

With time and practice, we may start to feel subtler vibrations while chanting. There is no way to know when this will occur and this experience would be different for everyone, but at some point when we have been chanting for a time, we may begin to experience the subtle vibrations of the mantra, in addition to purely physical vibrations. We may start to feel energy in various chakras and such. If you start to feel this subtle vibration, and especially once the vibration comes up to the manipura chakra (below the rib cage in the upper abdomen), this can make chanting more enjoyable and one may find oneself wanting to chant throughout the day at times when it suits you. You can practice keeping the focus on the subtle vibrations of the mantra. You cannot try to make the feelings happen but as they happen you may observe them. Just notice and enjoy. You are here for bhukti and mukti and everything in between and it's ok if you enjoy the process of your own spiritual unfoldment – your own awakening process.

Chapter Four:
Quiet & Silent Chanting

On the other hand, you don't have to chant so loud. You just have to chant loud enough to make a good vibration. Let the sounds of the Sanskrit language vibrate through you and start the good work of purifying your system. You can chant at whatever volume suits you. But try to make a nice vibration at whatever volume you chant. You can let your voice be a little quieter. Maybe some time you will feel it comes naturally to chant a little quieter. If you hear people around and are concerned they might hear you, out of modesty, you can chant quietly.

Going out to do grocery shopping can be a very good time to practice quiet chanting. Of course you don't want to chant out loud as you walk through the parking lot at the store or push your cart looking for items. But you can practice chanting under your breath. You can make a few chants while you are still in your car after you park, out loud if you like, if you feel privacy, then start to take the chanting within, to yourself, to just under your breath. Practice feeling the vibration of the mantra wherever you feel it in your body as you chant. Practice feeling the vibration of the mantra as it gets subtler and quieter.

The grocery store is a beautiful place to practice chanting, just under your breath, so that nobody can really hear what you are saying, but you can still hear it and still feel the vibration. This is nice because while you could chant silently going through the store, you will have a high level of distraction due to the fact of shopping, and you may have to stop chanting at times, while you actually shop, but as you walk and push your cart and go from here to there, you may chant very quietly, like the sound of a bell. It's fun. When you stop chanting, probably the chanting will continue silently in your head, and you can return to chanting out loud but very quietly when you have more attention to devote to it (like when you are pushing your cart from here to there or reaching for the orange juice).

It's harder to make a subtle sound and maintain the quality of the vibration. On the other hand, even the breath without any vocal cord sounds has its own vibration, so even if you whisper the mantra, it has a vibration and if you say it silently, you can bring the vibration into the silence with you, and by focusing on your mantra in the silence, you can feel the vibration in a more subtle way.

If you have a guru or teacher who is guiding you, they will tell you if the mantra given is to be chanted aloud, quietly, or silently.

Some practices are specifically intended to be silent and others are meant to be chanted out loud, and sometimes your guru may give instruction to chant a certain mantra very quietly, almost like a whisper, just under the breath.

There is nothing wrong with chanting silently. In some schools of thought, it is said that to chant silently is the best, in a very quiet voice like whispering is second best, and out loud is third best. Actually, each kind of chanting has its own benefits and certain people might be more drawn to certain types of chanting. I have heard a lot of people say that the silent chanting is superior to chanting out loud. I have several things to say about this.

For one thing, chanting silently can also be considered more advanced. My Tantric Japa Yoga practice has been mostly done out loud. Some parts have been silent, and some parts very quiet like a whisper, but most, in truth, has been out loud, and I have enjoyed it all.

However, there are times when I have done silent chanting and it has been very powerful. Still, I cannot imagine how or why I would want to do all the beautiful chanting I have done silently.

There are a lot of uses for chanting the mantra silently or very quietly. For one thing, others can't hear you. If another person hears you chanting very quietly, in theory this should be quiet enough so they can't make out what you are saying. It should be loud enough to keep yourself engaged with the chanting and to keep your focus on the chanting.

Chanting silently can also bring a profound inner effect and in some ways it might even feel superior in its own way to chanting out loud, because the focus can be very intense when one is chanting inwardly. If one can carry the vibration into the inner self on silent chanting, this can bring a very strong result and the vibration moves to a more subtle level, in that it does not make any gross physical sound, but on the inner level it can blossom out in a plume of vibration that feels very bright and golden and blissful.

First of all, if you are chanting on your own, you can do whatever you like, but if you are chanting for a guru, you should follow the instructions given by your guru because there are various styles of meditation and some are silent. I believe in starting with the sounded and getting grounded in that first, and my training and practice have been mostly with chanting out loud.

Silent Chanting: A Personal Experience

I had an experience involving silent chanting that for me was very profound. I was taking an advanced training with a high up teacher whom I respect. I had a difficult history with this teacher, by no fault of her own. I had been going through a time of my life, some years before, while I took a different training from her, and I was experiencing mania at that time. I wrote her quite a volume of daily email comments, which felt imperative at the time, due to my strong inner compulsion, due to anxiety & PTSD from trauma, and the difficulties my life was giving me at that time. Thankfully she's a very understanding person, never held it against me, and I was always welcome in her trainings. So I was going to an advanced training with this teacher, and I had grown a lot, and I wanted to be sure to get it all right. I didn't want to let myself get triggered and revert to old patterns. One therapist had recommended to me I move on from that teacher because I felt triggered by her. I wasn't buying any of that. I wanted to take this teacher's course; and still, I felt a little bit nervous about it.

So I started to chant the mantra – in this case it was Gayatri Mantra I was chanting – not part of any assignment I was doing at the time, just one of my mantras and I was chanting it. (See Chapter Ten for Gayatri Mantra). I just started to chant it in the morning, and I kept chanting it while I got ready for my course each day. Chanting would start out loud and slowly become quieter until I was in the classroom and chanting became silent. I had to focus so strongly in my will to keep the vivid focus inwardly on the mantra, on its sounds and in dhyana contemplation on its meanings as I chanted silently, and all the subtle vibrations being activated within me as I chanted, carried me through, charging me up. I continued this way through the first part of each day. At some point the focus of the class would force me to stop even my inward chanting, and by that time I was transported to another plane, very focused and on top of my game for the entire course. A number of times, I was the one who had the right answer in class, much to my delight, because I love to please a good teacher. I made it through the training without being triggered at all, in all pleasantness and light. And I learned something about the beauty, utility, and importance of silent chanting.

Practicing Samadhi, Cultivating Silence

Sometimes I fall silent.

At the end of the practice the silence enters in. There may be a slight sensation of lingering vibration in the head from all the vibration of chanting, or maybe a bright and a light feeling. One may feel more peaceful – more calm and detached. It's as if the vibrations of the chanting (and the breathing), wash the system clean and one has the feeling of being refreshed – pranafied. And at this time, one can do what is called practicing samadhi, or simply put, just rest in those feelings of peaceful contentment and let yourself linger and enjoy those feelings for a few minutes after meditation. This is called practicing samadhi.

Samadhi is another name for the blissful feeling of spiritual enlightenment, which is the state of consciousness one achieves when one realizes oneness with the Absolute –– when Shiva and Shakti unite in the crown chakra.

When the kundalini pierces through the third knot or granthi in the third-eye/ajna chakra, rising up into the crown, where she unites with Shiva/Consciousness, this is called awakening. One can have kundalini activated and processing through sushumna and the chakras, and one may feel a process, and experience awakening in little doses. And it has been reported that eventually one experiences in the end, a sudden explosion of energy and light in the head, and a feeling of deep peace that abides and never leaves, and this is final awakening. Then one is jivamukti or liberated (from the cycle of rebirth) while living.

This peaceful state of consciousness one achieves where one feels at one with it all and a sort of transcendental peace, is called Samadhi.

Samadhi is the state one achieves in the final awakening. However there are stages of Samadhi and we can catch glimpses of what these feelings of peacefulness are like, even if they don't stay forever. So, if you find yourself in such a state, you should enjoy it, and this is called practicing Samadhi. And you can practice Samadhi at the end of your Tantric Japa Yoga practice. We practice Samadhi also for some moments between each of the three, minute long rounds of kapalbhati pranayama (which is given and explained in Chapter Three): we pause for some moments before we do the next minute of breathing. Just rest and experience the good energy and be in Samadhi – practice letting it linger.

You can also practice samadhi as you go about your day if you are chanting and you have built the energy and you are feeling so full of your mantra, and suddenly you may find yourself having fallen silent: just enjoy it. Enjoy the moments of stillness. Enjoy the feeling of peace and calm and silence that fills you up and fills the air all around you, especially when you have been chanting or doing pranayama. Relax and observe the beauty in your surroundings, the natural aspects, trees, and the sound of the breeze. Experience what it is like to feel samadhi as you go about your day, instead of feeling stressed and hurried.

If you are doing your daily practice, you must do it. And if you are chanting in between your daily practice as you go about your day, chant as you need to chant. Chant when you think of it. Chant when you feel like it and chant when it makes sense, but don't make yourself chant if you feel like stopping, if it is stressing you out or giving you a headache. Just let yourself stop and enjoy going about your day.

Notice the peaceful feelings you feel when you have done some chanting and the silence rushes back in, and let yourself see if you can prolong that feeling a little bit, even as you go about your day. Over time, you will find that the peaceful feelings will last longer.

Sounds of Silence and Song

Silence rushes in after chanting. Really, we are so rarely in true, total silence. Silence is generally relative. Even if you get very silent in a super quiet space, you may start to hear the sound of your breath, or the sound of your heart-beat pounding in your ears. Some say that in the silence one can hear the universe humming Om in the heart. When you are out in the world, and you have been chanting and you fall silent, the silence around you will be relative. It's more of a quality, where you are more tuned in and silent, and you may even hear sounds more distinctly, and each of the sounds you hear will be more like a bell ringing in silence. Silence is like the container: sounds are cradled in an aura of silence, as your senses have been cleaned by the vibrations of your chanting. It's hard to describe what is meant by the silence, if you start to consider how sounds never stop, but if you are chanting in a place where there is some sound, and you stop, you can listen to the quality of your experience – how the quality even of the sounds you hear has changed somewhat. Of course there are limits to this: for instance, if you are surrounded by loud music, that is drowning everything out, and you can't even hear yourself chant. But sometimes you can, even when distractions are many, find your way into some simple mantra, or just let out a few "Om," very quietly. Make the vibration, feel the beautiful vibration, and try to find that peaceful feeling, wherever you are in your day.

If you are chanting out loud for a while, you might start to experience it as irritation and feel a desire to chant more quietly – then more quietly again until you are really finding your way into the subtle vibration of the mantra, and it just pings in you and it's so nice. So let yourself chant quietly or silently and experience how that can help you bring more peace and calm into your days.

The other day, I was at the gym, doing my cardio workout on my favorite cardio machine. A couple of ladies on machines next to me started talking about some political topic that was stressing me out because it was the aftermath of a very contentious election and my favorite candidate had lost. I opened my mouth and out came a few "OOOOOMMM Namah Shivaya. Ooooommm Namah Shivaya. Oooooommm Namah Shivaya." Three times I chanted it, and not too loudly, just sort of to myself but loud enough so if they were paying attention maybe they might hear. Then I fell silent. The ladies stopped their political chat, and became quiet and reflective as they pedaled, and I felt relief and calm, and finished my workout. I have been chanting mantra a lot in the gym under my breath. I think nobody can hear me, but I am carrying that energy with me. I can't really chant so much while I'm doing the cardio machine, as I am breathing rhythmically with the effort: it might work for you but for me it doesn't work to do chanting on the cardio machine. But I do other things at the gym and for those things I can chant under my breath, at least between sets. It keeps the useless ruminating out of my mind and helps me maintain a bright and focused energy.

Enjoy the silences in between your chanting. Don't try to make yourself chant all day if it's stressing you out. Just do your assignment and be done with it and enjoy the samadhi at the end of your practice. And as you are going about your day, if you find yourself in a moment of silence, pause. Feel your feet on the floor. Hear the sounds. See your surroundings afresh. Take a deep inhale and an exhale. Feel your breath move within you, and enjoy the silence.

Chapter Five:
Kundalini Shakti,
The Power Within You

In Tantra, Kundalini is Shakti/energy that rises up through sushumna to meet consciousness in the crown of the head to create enlightenment.

Kundalini is a word that is surrounded with a lot of mystery. Kundalini is Goddess Shakti, and in her form as Kundalini, she is called Kundalini Shakti. As Kundalini Shakti, the Goddess, or the Mother – the Divine Mother, as she is lovingly known – is the energy of all creation.

Kundalini exists at the base of the spine and is said to coil like a snake three and a half times around. Kunda is like a hollowed out crucible that holds something else, and the energy rests in there until it is awakened, at which point it makes its way upward, through each of the chakras, purifying the chakras as it goes, often taking its time over a process that can last years.

In *The Call of MahaShakti Mother Divine*, by Ratna Ma Navaratnam, the author says:

> "The Gayatri Mantra stimulates us to meditate on the sakti seated in the lotus inside the solar plexus. The lotus symbolizes a yogic chakra in the path of

Kundalini, situated along the spinal canal." "...thus all those who are initiated into the Gayatri Mantra are expected to lead a life geared to the living experience of Brahman." (p. 112-113)

A life geared to the living experience of Brahman, is a life geared to uncovering the true inner self, which is one with Brahman or in Tantric terms, one with Shiva, one with Mother Divine, one with ultimate consciousness and energy, as Kundalini Shakti unites with Shiva in the crown.

Kundalini Shakti is a ball of energy at the base of the spine, and when she is activated, she makes her way up the spine, working out the knots, and purifying the chakras, one by one, until she reaches the crown chakra at the top of the head, and one experiences, eventually, final awakening, or the realization of the self as one with Brahman, one with Lord Shiva, one with Divine Mother. This energy can rise all at once, suddenly, or can take its time: can rise in little doses and go up in little bursts, then go back down again, many times, over time, before one day making its big, dramatic final rise to the crown, where it may stay forever, or sometimes taking up residence in the heart.

All the various names of the divine point to one phenomenon, one God, one Absolute, that is beyond our scope of understanding, and which consists of consciousness and energy, in an ever intertwined state. All the names of the deities are various manifestations, roles, and portrayals of the cosmic energy, which is God.

We tend to think of God as something we can name. But the named aspects of God which are personified as quasi human forms, are created for our sake, so we can relate to the unfathomable ultimate reality in a way that feels more familiar. In fact, we are one energy with the divine at our core and all our lifetimes of evolution are to bring us to this ultimate realization on the inner realms that we are of one stuff with the cosmic divine.

Kundalini Shakti is a very specific energy that is within the human system and is situated at the base of the spine, at muladhara or the root chakra. However, prana is also circulating through the system. If prana were not circulating through our system, we would not be alive. And if Kundalini Shakti, as the static ground of our being, were not taking up residence in the muladhara (root) chakra, we would not be alive; she is an infinite source of energy and cannot be exhausted; she is the Divine Mother herself. Prana, or Pranashakti as she is known, is also the Divine Mother: as highly conscious energy, she flows through our 72,000 nadis, as well as through the two of the three main nadis in the body, ida and pingala, which weave their way through all six of the chakras up to ajna, the third-eye or brow chakra. As Pranashakti moves through our chakras, activating and enlivening, causing us to grow spiritually, so does kundalini, once activated, move through our chakras causing us to grow spiritually. However, Kundalini Shakti moves only in the sushumna nadi, the central channel that rises in a straight line from the base to the crown; Pranashakti moves in our chakras through ida and pingala nadis, but she does not move in sushumna, which is solely for Kundalini Shakti. A life geared toward experiencing Bhraman is a life geared toward activating these energies in us to bring us to the place within where we realize our oneness with absolute consciousness.

As we grow and evolve, our chakras begin to open a little with each new stage of our growth, and we are able to process more prana into our systems – or more kundalini – depending on what stage we are at – giving us more energy, and making us more conscious and intuitive. However there is a point at which the central nadi, sushumna, starts to open, and kundalini starts to travel up this central pathway, and this generally entails more energy and accelerated growth. Kundalini Shakti supports our well-being and our spiritual and personal growth. She is Mother Divine or the Divine Mother, and she is intelligent energy.

When Kundalini Shakti makes her way up the sushumna nadi, her ultimate goal is to unite with Shiva in the crown of the head. This union creates enlightenment, and can happen little by little, over time, until a final big union takes place and then Shakti never leaves, bringing a permanent expansion of consciousness.

As for prana, the sun is one very important source of prana for us. The sun is such a powerful ball of light. Sun has its own prana and it wakes up all life on the earth. It is said we have an inner sun that wakes us up, that manifests as light inside us. Ayurvedically there is also tejas inside of us – the inner fire – that brings luster to the skin and the aura and brightness to our being, as well as being responsible for aspects of our physical functioning and brings luster to the countenance. Being charged up with prana is good for us and we are responsible for guarding our prana. In fact, if prana is depleted, kundalini cannot be activated.

In Hinduism and in Tantra, there is a lot of shapeshifting. Brahman is the ultimate except when there is Shiva, then Shiva is the ultimate and Shiva is Brahman, except when there is Shakti, then Shakti is the ultimate and Shakti is Brahman. And Shiva is Shakti.

There is this constant interplay among the deities who have names and countenances we can relate to, and the Ultimate – the infinite beyond conception. Kundalini Shakti is one more case of this, and we find that Kundalini Shakti is one of the names of God.

Shri Mataji Nirmala Devi has stated, "Kundalini is our Mother, we are Her only children and She has been with us through all our lives just waiting for the moment of fulfillment."[2]

Lots of things in life cause kundalini to awaken. First of all, we are evolving over millions of years and slowly learning. If we do a lot of things and try everything we can, just to wake up the kundalini, and try certain techniques, it has been reported that kundalini rising can be sudden and intense. Kundalini rising doesn't have to happen suddenly. Kundalini can take its time rising through the chakras and we can have time in our lives to process. Some processes, such as TJY, are designed to pace the process, so that it does happen a little bit at a time.

Of course, nobody can really control kundalini or make her activate herself, or make her rise to the crown, or make her stop if she decides to rise. She has a mind of her own and therefore it is said that there is an element of grace involving kundalini activation and rising. However, taking the sensible path will more likely yield a more predictable result. Gopi Krishna is I think a good example. He meditated alone without the support of any tradition or guru, meditating on a single perfected and beautiful image of a lotus flower. By his own report he focused all his energy into visualizing one static image, sustained over a long period of time. Then he experienced a very powerful explosion of energy that was too much for him, was very difficult for him to process, and

---

[2] (www.sahajayoga.org).

by his own report, was detrimental to his health. Other forms of meditation might not create that sort of result. In Tantric Japa Yoga, there is not such a concentrated focus on one static image: the focus shifts and moves around a lot, sometimes from one phase to another, and also farther on in the practice, there can be a lot of movement just within a single practice, such as the tarpanams and nyasas. Also the mind is always learning more as the stories unfold. And as they unfold they teach certain knowledge about the subtle body that gives us a conceptual framework that can make us a more conscious container for kundalini energy and experience.

If you don't like the results you are getting from meditation, or they are too intense, you can always take a few days off from meditating. Even if you aren't experiencing kundalini energy, sometimes we just need time to grow and evolve, and if you need a break from meditation, enjoy the silence and find other ways to go within and honor your soul processes that nurture you through it.

If you want to experience accelerated spiritual growth, you can always go to an ashram where you have access to a guru and other spiritual people who have been through the same thing and can offer encouragement and advice. Then in an ashram you won't be bothered by the dramas or responsibilities of daily life and can focus on your spiritual unfoldment. If kundalini is raised too fast with techniques and when kundalini rises fast, it can cause emotional upheavals and other complications, because you are causing yourself to evolve faster and may create a bumpy ride.

In Tantra, we can be a "householder" or somebody with a worldly life and even a family, involved in the world, and we can still at the same time follow a spiritual path and achieve spiritual growth and awakening, all the way up to enlightenment, if it is our time to be enlightened.

So, if you just want to live your life and take your time, you can work with a tantric guru as I have done. This way you can take your time evolving, one phase at a time. Enjoy the ride. Learn as you go. Appreciate the beautiful unfolding of the stories embedded in the practices. And give your soul time to evolve instead of rushing things.

Practices in Tantric Japa Yoga can and do activate kundalini, and a lot depends on you personally because no two people have the same experience. It is an individual experience, tailored to you, because it is what you need as you evolve and grow. Kundalini adds energy to things. It causes the chakras to open more and take on more energy flow which means it has to clear old blocks and samskara from the system.

And so it can happen that a person evolves over many lifetimes, sometimes opening sushumna and activating kundalini but not achieving moksha, in the previous life: then in their next lifetime they will come into life with the kundalini already activated to the degree it had activated in the previous lifetime; and still it can take years to rise, or even lifetimes, and make its final ascent in final awakening.

If you have a spiritual experience, prana may be involved in stirring up one of the chakras, or kundalini activity may be involved: once kundalini is activated in the person, the experience of energy in the body and in the chakras takes on a new quality, not experienced before the activation of Kundalini Shakti. The experiences that I have been having since kundalini started to be active, have their own quality, and are often experiences related to energy and consciousness in the body and mind.

Kundalini Experience

If I had been looking and waiting for kundalini all the time I was on the path, until now, I might have gotten frustrated and given up. But, I never thought about it, and one wants to create a neutral state of consciousness when meditating. Striving for enlightenment is not a neutral state: it's an ego state of desire and it results from agitation that comes from a dissatisfaction with the status quo and a feeling of grasping.

As soon as I started to experience it, and especially once I realized this was going to be a regular thing, I began to want to know more. One can find information on kundalini. But it can be very technical sometimes and hard to understand. Personally, I have enjoyed reading accounts that are more personal, such as of other people's experiences, and even read the results of a study by the National Institutes of Health, about people who meditate and have kundalini experiences. And for me I always want to know. Also, I want to vouch for the practices I am doing and let you know that they work, and they have worked and are working for me. So, I decided to share my personal journey regarding kundalini energy and spiritual experiences.

I've read what I have gotten my hands on and the feeling is still one of wanting to know more, which I suppose my experience will tell me over time. I am finding that along with going back to review my Tantric Japa lessons to remind myself of certain details, and with reading other peoples' reports and experiences, I have gotten the impression that people who meditate regularly and consistently for a long time, for ten years or longer, eventually may succeed in activating kundalini. Then they start to experience activated kundalini energy and if they continue to practice while experiencing activated kundalini, eventually this may lead to a full blown awakening; however, full blown kundalini awakenings are reportedly fairly uncommon. Yet, we should be aware of all the possibilities.

Since I have not experienced a full blown kundalini awakening, I cannot comment on it other than to report what I have learned from study. Most people are reporting, that eventually one experiences an explosion of energy and light into the head and a feeling of cosmic peace and bliss that changes one's perspective, and brings one to a non-dual state of being, where one realizes oneness with God consciousness, as well as oneness with all one's fellow beings and all of creation. Then one is jivamukti and still goes about one's life but feels a deep contentment and peace and has a different perspective inside.

Since I have been experiencing kundalini, I can feel the drift in this direction: I do feel more peace and contentment; I find myself smiling more; and I find myself just losing myself in the flow of my day, which is nice. Even recently, when we had a stressful reaction to the outcome of a political election here in the US, I had to deal with unexpected emotional turmoil in the home. I felt new resourcefulness and an inner confidence, peace and calm. I applied myself to the situation and felt kundalini energy rising in me in the midst of the upset, something I'd never experienced like that in my life. And when I gave a hands on marma treatment to a loved one (marma is a system of pressure points in the Hindu system, similar to Chinese pressure point therapy), and I silently chanted Gayatri Mantra in my head while administering the therapy, I felt the bright energy and light in the frontal part of my brain vibrating poignantly with the mantra as I chanted silently, and I felt surges of energy go through my hands into the receiver. Calm was restored, along with a feeling of relaxation. These things are all anecdotal, meaning, you have to take my word for it that I had a feeling of energy while I was using a hands-on form of therapy. This was my personal experience and probably one more reason why more people don't report their experiences up front, because the experience is inner experience and somebody else might not believe or appreciate it. In Tantra, we value our subjective experience.

Today, I felt kundalini stirring in me because my spouse had skin cancer removed from his ear, and I was feeling for him, as they had to take more than initially anticipated, and the follow up procedures are complicated. It's a relatively small surface wound on his ear that nonetheless goes down all the way to the cartilage and it's a big deal. It has to heal right. I let Om roll through me out loud on my voice and the feeling of tears welled up in my throat, moved through me, and released on the Om, as the sound of Om was expiring on my exhale. The vibration was strong in my brow, in ajna chakra, and it made me a little dizzy as I was consciously concentrating on the energy pulling up from heart to brow as I chanted just a few Om. My momentary sadness was massaged out of me, coaxed from my heart and rolled out over my throat on the Om. It's worth saying in this context, that when we get stressed out, it's typically the discursive mind that won't quiet down; however, when one chants mantra, and certain mantra may be more conducive to this than others, depending on the person and the moment, but when we chant, the discursive mind is put on pause, and the feelings then may flow. When feelings flow they heal. When feelings are stagnant we feel stuck.

Chakras and Kundalini

When kundalini starts to awaken in you, you may start at that time to feel energy in the chakras. When chanting or doing pranayama energy may be felt in various chakras. Energy may be felt in the base chakra during mantra japa and may rise up and diffuse into the belly region. Energy may rise up into the manipura chakra just below the rib cage and may feel very poignant there. Energy may rise up and start to vibrate and feel very nice in the heart, and sometimes, and even especially when finding one's way into the sweet vibration that can be there when we are chanting silently, energy may be felt in the brow chakra. Energy may be felt in the brow if you are chanting out loud too. But there is a special quality that I have experienced when I find my way to that silent or very quiet chanting and the subtle vibration of the mantra can be felt within: it can at times rise in a very pleasant way, like a rich full bulb of light pulsating into the brow chakra.

So when you feel the subtle energy pulsating in your various chakras, then you know that kundalini is doing her work, purifying your centers. And she has been there all along from the beginning, waiting, while prana went ahead of her and did all the preliminary work, purifying our past karmas and preparing the way for more positive changes.

Subtle Vibrations

Since kundalini has been activated in my system, I feel what I will call the subtle vibrations of the mantras, which is another way of saying thatI feel a sort of energy when chanting that I didn't notice before; it seems to me like subtle energy; and I feel these vibrations in my chakras.

Today I was out and about and I had a moment all to myself with nobody around and I let out a long plaintive *Om Namah Shivaya,* and I felt the energy rolling through my throat and out on the crest of the wave of the energy rolling through my throat chakra. I felt the feeling as if I might start to cry. I didn't even have a mental concept of what I was about to cry about.

It's not necessary to be so analytical with the self. It is good to be aware, and I'm glad the awareness of sadness moved through me over my throat chakra. I did some more chanting after that, as I was going through my day – "Om Namah Shivaya" – until I felt like my throat chakra was cleared of all the sad energy.

As I talk about it, part of me feels convicted that this is the right thing to do, but because all this energy is still new to me part of me feels a little nervous that if I talk about it, maybe it will leave me, or not return, or maybe I'm being premature and the energy is never going to come back. I don't experience it constantly, though some things are constant like a feeling of greater mental alertness and having an easier time remembering things I read. The energy, that is so enjoyable, sometimes reaches a pitch where it is so exquisite, and almost gives the feeling, as if the energy is expanding my soul in a way that feels cosmic, and beneficial, and impossible to describe, and I don't want this to stop.

Why am I grateful for the kundalini experience? Certainly, I always hankered for spiritual experience and enjoyed having spiritual experience whenever I had any.

But there is more to it than just that. I can honestly say, that the kundalini is dissolving whatever artifacts were lingering in my personality that had anything to do with suffering because of trauma, like PTSD. I used to find myself in certain mental states in certain situations even after years of therapy and meditating, and now, that has all melted away as if by magic. It seems that it's been melting away more noticeably since a few times I felt light shoot up into my head, and since I have been feeling the subtle vibration of the mantra. Even my therapist commented recently that she thought I was healing from trauma.

I find myself smiling more often. I find myself feeling more sensitive and tuned in to others. This all feels like a sort of magic, after working at everything consciously for years in therapy and feeling the painstaking slow progress. Doing inner-child work and really loving it and feeling it in the emotional body – how great it is – and doing all the left-right journaling in which left hand (non-dominant hand) expresses the strong feeling of the inner-child, and right hand responds as the ideal loving and wise parent. This encourages grounding into the body and learning to observe the sensations in the body behind the feelings, as well as reclaiming the self. Gratitude journaling also feeds the soul. It all helped and it all did me a lot of good and my therapist felt I have all the tools, and I was ready to graduate from therapy because I was "doing very well." And I was. But I still had some of the lingering artifacts of trauma in my system and it finally has just sort of faded away as kundalini energy has been taking a more active role in my life. I haven't quit therapy as if quitting a bad habit. I still schedule occasionally with my therapist if I have some unexpected rough spot and need help processing it all. In truth, kundalini can also stir up old stuck wounds for us to process and heal, so learning tools for emotional processing in therapy is good.

I encourage everyone to meditate if you think you would like to experience this someday and just know that it might take some time before you start to experience kundalini energy on a regular basis in your life. And maybe you will start to experience it much sooner than I did, because maybe you have a lot less baggage than I had, or for other reasons only Kundalini Shakti knows.

Siddhis

Siddhis are special powers and abilities that come to a person as a result of kundalini being active in the body, and especially as a result of kundalini awakening.

Usually what one hears is that one acquires siddhis with the movement of kundalini in sushumna. One doesn't hear so much what these siddhis might be. Giving pranic healing through the hands is one of the siddhis. The ability to give pranic healing is one of the gifts one may acquire with kundalini activation.

I am not going to try to enumerate all the siddhis or educate everyone on siddhis. But I will say this much. I think there are little siddhis and then there are big siddhis. Some of the littler siddhis have just to do with things like seeing auras or being able to sense things in a new way from Shiva Tattva (the Ultimate Reality or consciousness), and being able to do pranic healing.

Also, regarding certain siddhis, there is the matter of interpretation. For example: one siddhi is the ability to expand very large. Some interpret this to be expanding the body. But I have seen it also interpreted as expanding the subtle body. A memory comes to mind that seems related. I remember when my parents were at sea years ago. They were sailing by themselves as a team of two. We heard from them once every few weeks. One time in the middle of their several weeks long communication gap, I became worried. I felt an abstract sense of my parents as if their spirits had expanded to be very large, reaching down to the bottom of the waves, encompassing a large space around their boat. Later, when we heard from them, I learned that they had been in a very bad storm around that time. The waves had been so intense that my father was holding onto the helm standing on the side wall of the cockpit as the boat cut sideways through the big waves. They were afraid but they made it through the storm. Maybe the intensity of the situation activated their energies and gave them access to the siddhi of expansion so they could feel into sailing in the storm and stay safely afloat. Just speculating.

Some of the bigger siddhis, like walking on water or materializing things are not achieved by the vast majority of people. I have heard tell that in India some of the more isolated sadhus (spiritual aspirants) will only in very private situations ever reveal that they have such siddhis. I have not experienced it and so I will end my commentary here.

Chapter Six:
Pranashakti and Spiritual Growth.

Prana is universal energy, and is also known as Pranashakti, a very important aspect of Divine Mother. Pranashakti, or simply prana, is the life force which pervades our bodies through various means, including running itself through the 72,000 nadis or energy pathways in our bodies, and including two of three major nadis, ida and pingala. Prana, however, does not travel through sushumna nadi – the central channel – which is reserved for Kundalini Shakti.

Our breath carries prana, and prana is sort of like the breath. It is not exactly the breath, but rather the subtle dimension of the breath. Breathing brings fresh prana into our bodies via oxygen. Sunlight brings fresh prana into our bodies. Eating fresh healthy food brings prana into our bodies. Yoga asana (postures), meditation practices and pranayama all increase prana.

Good sleep charges us up with prana. In fact, sleep has its own special way to refresh prana within us, because it is said that when we are in the deep sleep state, we are back in the state where we are one with Lord Shiva or absolute consciousness. When we are in deep sleep there is no awareness of the external world, and it is very refreshing because we go back to the original state. As soon as we wake up in the morning we begin our day having to make choices, about this to do and that to do, and the soul snaps into an active state. But in the deep sleep state there is a total letting go: there is no striving, nor any choices to make; and one is in a state of oneness with absolute consciousness or Lord Shiva, which is very refreshing. Thus when we get good deep sleep, we wake up refreshed and energized, or pranafied.

Prana also supports tejas and ojas in the body. Tejas is the subtle form of fire or pitta, while ojas is the subtle form of kapha, or earth and water, and prana is the subtle form of air or vata. Prana, tejas, and ojas are Ayurvedic properties that keep us healthy and alive. Ayurveda is an ancient holistic health science that is a sister science to yoga. In later TJY practices that I have learned, and am learning, I have seen that there is some overlap and interplay between concepts and powers, between Ayurveda and Tantric Cosmology. There are specific yoginis, for instance, in charge of specific dhatus or body tissues. A yogini is a ray of light from Goddess Shakti. Having more prana in the body nourishes ojas and tejas in the body and thereby improves our vitality.

Prana is universal energy and she is also another name for the Goddess Shakti: She is called Pranashakti, because prana is energy. When we say prana is energy we mean energy is the dominant expression but it is always energy with consciousness, because prana is energy with a lot of intelligence. Without consciousness, the energy doesn't have a direction or a purpose. Without consciousness it is only potential energy.

Pranayama or breathing practices are one way to work on prana in the body. Working on prana in the body through pranayama creates movement of prana in the body through the nadis. Prana moves through the nadis in the body and pranayama gets the prana moving in certain ways and sometimes moving more. Prana moving through ida and pingala nadis passes through the chakras and can activate chakras and create certain kinds of spiritual experience. Pranayama stirs up prana which can activate kundalini over time. And mantra japa also raises prana in the body.

Pranayama and chanting are two ways to generate tapas, which is the heat created from practice, and feeds tejas in the body, which could be seen as an expression of the inner sun – inner luminosity. All these things have the power to stimulate kundalini and still, from my own experience and from reports of others that I have read, sometimes pranayama can trigger energy, but usually it takes a longer time and more than a few weeks of practice to trigger kundalini activation. Kundalini has a mind of its own and will activate when it is ready, and yet some practices can bring us along the path in the direction of kundalini activation.

When kundalini is not being activated, purification is still taking place in the chakras. The three main nadis all run through the chakras. The three main nadis are ida, pingala, and sushumna. Ida and pingala weave, in sort of like a wave pattern, from the base chakra through all the chakras to the third-eye, or ajna chakra, in between the eye-brows in the middle of the forehead. Ida and pingala nadis circulate prana through the chakras up to the sixth chakra or ajna chakra in the brow. And sushumna nadi goes up in a straight line from the base chakra to the crown chakra and this chakra is the one that kundalini travels in when it awakens, processing its way through all the chakras, one by one, until it finally breaks through the third knot in the third-eye and rises all the way up to the crown or sahasrara chakra, in an explosion. Prana does not travel in sushumna nadi: only kundalini travels in sushumna nadi.

The nadis are energy pathways that carry prana throughout the body and there are 72,000 nadis.

The chakras are like energy vortexes, and the three primary nadis run through them.

Chakras

Up until now, I have not discussed the chakra system in detail and I do not want to spend too much time on the chakras, because this subject has been dealt with by others in great detail, and you can always reference those works. I will give a brief list of some details pertaining to each chakra.

A chakra is an energy center in the body. The six main chakras, and the seventh (which is sometimes not considered a chakra), sahasrara (the crown chakra), all align vertically along the spine, and are also represented in Tantra as flowers, each having a specific number of petals, with each petal containing a letter of the Sanskrit alphabet. Chakras pull energy of the cosmos into the body and form the energetic field around the body that we call the aura.

I do believe the chakras exist and are real. But by real I mean that I have learned and I believe that they exist on a subtle, spiritual level, not within the actual structure of the physical body. They are contained within the space of the physical body, but they could not be cut out of it. Our chakras contain energy about us, about who we are, where we come from and where we are going. Chakras hold us energetically in being.

I have been feeling energy in my chakras as I have been doing my practices, now that I have been experiencing Kundalini Shakti as the subtle vibrations of the mantra – and subtle vibrations in general. However, I need to let you know that my experience is evolving. I think it's important to talk about this experience somewhat, and in part because more often than not, people don't. Actually you can find a fair amount online scouring the chat pages, but in books, most people tend to keep their personal experience out of it. I feel like including my personal experience because it is what I have to learn from and others can learn from my experience as I have learned from the stories I've read from other people – travelers on the path.

I have been experiencing the chakras and I think they are real, and there is every reason why it might make sense that they could be. After all, our physical body has vital organs and major centers of activity. In Ayurvedic terms, we have what are called the seven dhatus or body tissues, such as the skin, the blood, the muscles, the fat and etc. Also, we have the sub-doshas of the ayurvedic dosha system. These are ways that our body operates by organizing itself around certain functions. For instance we have a circulatory system, also called the cardiovascular system, that revolves around the fact that we breathe and circulate oxygen, and that our heart pumps and circulates blood. It consists of a heart, and veins that run around the body and through and back to the heart. We have a lymphatic system also, and a musculo-skeletal system – all things that define the structure and function of our physical body. It makes sense that on the spiritual level there would also be centers of focus for the function of our individual soul as it experiences life in the body.

What I have experienced is energy in the base chakra, energy in the second chakra, swadhisthana. I have felt energy in the solar plexus, energy in the heart, a very subtle and pleasant refined energy in the throat, which is subtle and not so quickly noticed unless I focus on it. I have noticed vibrations in the third-eye and in the crown. I also experienced clearing a blocked throat chakra by chanting ham, the bija for vishuddhi, into the throat chakra. I have breathed and chanted into the third-eye, heart, and crown at times.

Why do I consistently feel energy in these places? There must be something there – something going on – I don't feel energy in my left eyebrow, for instance. Just in the center between the eyebrows. I don't feel the vibration in my left arm. I feel it in my heart. I don't feel the energy in my right knee, I feel it in the circle of the belly that contains swadhisthana chakra.

So yes, I do believe the centers exist, and I take it as given that information about these chakras has been passed down through time, and has evolved somewhat, and also stayed mostly the same.

There are seven chakras. In the tantric system, each of the chakras has a flower in it with a specific number of petals and the letters of the Sanskrit alphabet are placed one by one on each of the petals of the chakras. In TJY there are a variety of practices that involve meditating on the chakras, which one may do and familiarize oneself with the energy of the chakras.

There are seven chakras from bottom to top:

1. **Base, or muladhara chakra**, rules our earthiness, and feelings of security and belonging in the world. It is also where kundalini resides.
   Color is red.
   Element is Earth.
   Bija Mantra is Lam.

2. **Swadhisthana, or the sacral chakra** is our feelings, emotions, creativity and our sexuality.
   Color is orange.
   Element is Water.
   Bija Mantra is Vam.

3. **Manipura, or the solar plexus chakra**, in the abdomen above the belly button and below the ribs, is our sense of purpose in life and how we fit in socially. Color is yellow.
   Element is Fire.
   Bija Mantra is Ram.

4. **Anahata, or the heart chakra** is in the chest and is our ability to give and receive love. It is green in color. The heart chakra is also connected to the hands: there is a big chakra in the center of the palm of each hand; this is why lovers hold hands, because it is a direct connection to the heart. It is also how healers effect hands on healing, as they channel the energy of prana through their hands as their heart chakras align with prana through whatever mantra they are chanting while doing hands-on healing. One can use the Gayatri Mantra for hands-on healing.
   Color is Green.
   Element is Air.
   Bija Mantra is Yam.

5. **Vishuddi , or the throat chakra**, governs psychic abilities as well as our freedom in expressing ourselves. This chakra is related to Vak devi, and the capacity to create through the power of speech.
   Color is blue.
   Element is Ether.

Bija Mantra is Ham.

6. **Ajna, or the famous third-eye chakra,** is between the eyebrows. Ajna is the command center, is very active in sexuality, is a focal point in meditation, and the more active and open ajna is, the more sushumna opens and can carry more kundalini.
Color is indigo.
Element is the MahaTattva, which contains all the other elements within it, in their subtle aspect.
Bija Mantra is Om.

7. **Crown chakra, or sahasrara,** is our spiritual self, at the top of the head, and is where we feel our connection to divinity, as well as being where Shiva and Shakti, consciousness and energy, unite in final awakening.
Color is Violet.
Element is pure spirit.
Bija Mantra is Om.

We can meditate on the chakras and become more aware of them, and sometimes we can notice ourselves feeling from them. The most obvious is that when we are very sad we are said to feel a heaviness of heart. Or sometimes in meditation we may feel ajna chakra vibrating.

Spiritual Growth

When we wake up prana, it is good for us – it helps us wake up and grow spiritually. Prana can respond right away to chanting and pranayama. The energy of the guru can also activate prana. It's happened more than once, that after meeting with Shajesh on Zoom to discuss a new assignment, I go do my practice and I find that I feel a real boost in energy and find myself chanting more fluently; and it usually wears off after a few days.

We have prana flowing through our bodies and it keeps us alive. We can be prana depleted, just like we can be energy depleted. After all, prana is energy: energy with consciousness.

We can be prana depleted or we can be filled up with ample, fresh, prana, filled and overflowing with good energy – with prana. In fact it is our job to guard or own prana, and prevent it from being drained out of us.

Situations that drag us down with negativity and unnecessary drama can deplete our prana. Situations that feed and support our various systems increase our prana.

Kundalini takes longer to respond than prana. And once the kundalini starts to be activated you can feel it moving in your body, in your chakras, and in your life, erasing old complexes and fears and making you fresh again. And once this starts to happen, don't stop practicing; keep on practicing day after day.

As we breathe and chant, the vibrations are stimulating prana. This is a good thing for our spiritual growth, because instead of reinforcing negative thoughts and patterns in the brain, that drain prana, we are replacing them with good energy and a focus on the divine. Meanwhile the process of meditation reduces activity in the limbic center, the part of the brain that worries about stress, and strengthens the part of the brain that is pro-active about dealing with life.

Just think of all the tapes you will not be running of worry about this or that. If some thought about this or that enters your mind, you can just keep chanting and let the thought go to the Divine, and the energy will be raised up by chanting, instead of letting your mind be dragged down in worries that can create negative self-fulfilling prophecies.

How many times have you awakened from sleep to find the lines of some song going through your head? Just any old song from the radio? It almost becomes like a mantra. And studies show that repeating the same words over and over reduces stress in the brain because of how it deactivates the discursive mind. However, meanwhile we could be creating a groove in our brain by chanting mantra, with information about consciousness and creation, the Divine Mother, or the Sun, while we raise our prana. And even better yet, what if our minds find a new degree of stillness, and in stillness we may find that samadhi. Chanting and pranayama are both practices which increase prana and feed the soul.

After a while, when you have been chanting and wearing a deep groove in your mind, of devotion, of contemplation on deep spiritual truths that point you in the direction of your inner self and you get tired of making so much noise, you can let it fall off and just stop chanting for a while and enjoy the silence, or chant quietly and work with that energy, or try chanting silently. When you have had enough, your mind will fall silent and should be energized and refreshed. Instead of meaningless chatter, you will have mantra floating through your mind with a feeling of reverence to higher realities and devotion to deep truths.

And you don't have to do any extra chanting at all, if you don't want to, or it if doesn't work out that way. Just continue your daily practice. Enjoy the added degree of stillness and detachment you feel as a result of practicing. Keep finding time each day for your regular practice, enjoy the lift in prana you may experience, and don't worry about the rest.

Dhyana & Other Practices

Dhyana and other meditative practices also increase prana.

Dhyana is a practice you can also do when you are not chanting, when you feel like being in silence but still want to meditate. Dhyana is a way to meditate by contemplating spiritual verses or songs. You can also contemplate your life, and this can be a form of self-study as well as cultivating the inner-witness.

Contemplation is not the same as discursive thinking. Discursive thinking is problem oriented – focused on solving problems and discussing issues. Contemplation is the free flowing imagination when it is activated around a specific topic, and it can also bring insight. Contemplation is more like a dance where you twirl and spin around, and there is no goal but the dance itself. Contemplation springs from a still mind, whereas discursive thinking is analytical, and springs from a busy mind that has a lot to get done. Discursive thinking is like walking across the floor to sit in a chair or putting away the dishes – getting something done. Contemplation is a form of reflection that is more like active dreaming.

Another practice is called antar mouna, and involves watching the activity of one's mind and thoughts, which is a way to establish the inner-witness.

Tantric Japa Yoga has chanting, the japa, and one can also incorporate dhyana, antar mouna, even journaling and working with a psychologist to learn to know and master the self as a form of svadhyaya – self-study and/or study of sacred scriptures. Tantric Japa Yoga brings one to a place where one has, over time, more and more jnana, or spiritual knowledge and wisdom, because one spends more time contemplating and exploring all the themes one has been chanting about. Combining spiritual practices supports prana and can help us grow and evolve.

The Beauty and Utility of Tantric Japa Yoga

Tantric Japa Yoga is a great program for spiritual development, precisely because it is a great program for stimulating prana within us.

You can try to meditate and evolve by just taking Om Namah Shivaya as your mantra and going through your life with that. No matter how many times you chant the same mantra over and over, it will still continue to stimulate your prana day after day.

Or you can stop with Phase Two, incorporating Om Gayatri Om into your regular practice, and let all that be your practice throughout your life. No matter how many times you do the Phase Two practices they will always continue to awaken prana in you, day after day. And this will contribute to your spiritual unfolding.

You can do any form of meditation that consists of chanting some single syllable vibration in the silence of your mind, or out loud. It will feed prana within you. It can lead you toward enlightenment.

And if you want to learn tantric cosmology, doing so will take you farther on the path of spiritual growth, as the positive mental stimulation of such study will elevate the mind and increase the activity of prana within. TJY gives a whole study in tantric cosmology.

It will increase your efforts to combine all the types of practice, which means learning more. We say often how important it is to keep learning in life, and the same is true in the spiritual life. Learning more about spiritual realities and concepts that bring us to feelings of reverence and devotion, can help us evolve spiritually and bring us closer to the goal of moksha.

Tantric Japa Yoga is like a beautiful story unfolding and it will give you plenty to study and contemplate, beyond the minutes you spend chanting each day, so there are a variety of ways in which TJY increases prana within us and this makes it a great program for spiritual development.

Pranayama: Breathing Exercises

Pranayama, or conscious breathing exercises, are practiced in TJY and are another one of the tools we can use to begin to bring our attention within – to move closer to our true nature, beyond duality, beyond the discursive mind. And pranayama is a way to fortify prana within the body and mind.

In deep sleep, our soul relaxes and we are one with Shiva in the pure state. We recharge. As soon as we are awake we have to make choices and our soul springs into action: it literally tenses like a ping, as it moves through the day making one choice after another. And this is ok but we become too identified with the external actions and forget our inner self. We need to become more subjective and aware of what is going on inside of us, and less objective or aware of objects that are external to us. Pranayama is one of the tools for helping us move close to connect with the inner self, as the discursive mind is stilled and falls away.

We tend to think of the breathing exercises as good for the lungs and they are – as good for relaxation and they are. But they are also good at activating energy. Pranayama gets the pranic energy currents moving within us, activates prana in the body, and has the power with continued practice to activate the kundalini coiled at the base of the spine, which leads to enlightenment.

Pranayamas can be intense, some more-so than others, and can accelerate the activation of kundalini. By slowing our Phase One pranayama down and doing the kapalbhati breathing in three segments, this makes it so that the practice is not too activating all at once. Also, we get to really appreciate feeling samadhi that the pranayama brings, when we pause between the minutes of breathing.

We always get the feeling that we are doing pranayama for our personal well-being, and we are. Pranayama has a variety of benefits.

One of the benefits of pranayama is spiritual growth because pranayama works not just the breath and the lungs, but the prana, the conscious, life-force energy of the body, which runs through the 72,000 nadis or energy pathways in our body, as well as through our chakras, via ida and pingala nadis, energizing us and raising our vibration, purifying our elements and eventually over time creating the heat and friction necessary to activate Kundalini Shakti.

Pranayama is one more tool to keep ourselves growing and evolving spiritually.

Part Two: Practices

Introduction to Part Two:

Part Two is about practices. I have done my best to take a broad view of this and give the reader plenty of help understanding content and meaning of key mantras and practices, of the characters who appear in them, and how they all fit into the broader picture of tantric cosmology.

Chapters Seven and Eight give the actual practices from Tantric Japa Yoga: Phases One and Two, respectively. This is a real gift to the reader, and a revelation from the heart of a substantial tantric lineage.

Chapters Nine and Ten explore Phases Three and Four of TJY, exploring related characters and themes from tantric cosmology. A few mantras are given for the lone practitioner who may wish to experiment on their own.

Chapter Eleven explores the Divine Mother and gives a glimpse of some of the TJY practices that feature various goddesses.

Chapter Seven:
TJY Phase One:
Om Namah Shivaya

When I met Shajesh, the first thing he said to me was, "Do you want me to teach you Tantric Japa Yoga?" And I said, right away, without thinking, in one of those blink moments, "Sure."

I might have responded more enthusiastically, but it was a response in the affirmative that seemed to rise from the depths of me in an instant, and went forth from me in an aura of certitude. Sometimes I have a hard time making decisions, but in this instance that was not the case. Somehow I knew on the spot that I should take Shajesh up on his offer, even though I didn't really know what Tantric Japa Yoga was.

Shajesh gave me my first assignment right away. My very first mantra straight from my Hindu Tantric Guru, was Om Namah Shivaya. And this is a fitting place to begin. Om Namah Shivaya is certainly a very popular mantra that has been chanted millions of times, over thousands of years, by millions of people. It is a very powerful, beautiful and beneficial mantra, and it is simple: only three words:

Om Namah Shivaya

Om Namah Shivaya is a simple mantra, considering the fact that it has only three words, and all are easy to pronounce for people who are not familiar with Sanskrit sounds yet. Om Namah Shivaya is also very profound and carries, in a nutshell, a basic premise of Tantric spirituality: Lord Shiva is consciousness; and Shiva, who is consciousness, is the one to whom we are bowing, or acknowledging with reverence and respect, as God.

Om: Pranava: Original Vibration

Before we go further, let's take a look at Om, since Om is the first word of the mantra Om Namah Shivaya.

Om is a very profound word in Sanskrit.

In Hinduism and in Tantra, Om is actually the original word, and in fact Om is the original vibration, the original cosmic sound. In fact, one could say that Om is God, beyond any thought name or concept: just vibration. The first cosmic vibration, Om, is called the pranava and is God, and emanates from God, or the Divine Mother, which is consciousness and energy – moving. The first cosmic vibration, Om, emanates out of Lord Shiva, who is consciousness, when he is excited by Divine Mother Shakti. On the one hand, Shiva is consciousness and on the other hand, Lord Shiva is God.

Tantric cosmology is complicated. There is the original Brahman and Brahman is beyond all form – the vast incomprehensible All underlying the phenomenal world is Brahman. Then from Brahman we distinguish Shiva and Shakti, or consciousness and energy respectively. In reality, the two, Shiva and Shakti, are united in a constant cosmic interplay. In principle, they are one and the same, but as we consider them, and as they start to distinguish themselves in the process of creation, they separate out as Shiva and Shakti, consciousness and energy. Either one of them may be considered Brahman, and the one is never really separated from the other.

Shiva is inert consciousness without Shakti and yet he is never separated from Shakti. It is as a result of Shakti, that Shiva or consciousness, starts to move in the form of a vibration.

When consciousness makes its initial vibration, that is the Om vibration, and it is the original sound that all other sounds emanate from. Om is the audible form of the nada, the very subtle, cosmic vibration of the universe, which is beyond our physical ears' ability to hear. This Om vibration starts as nada and evolves over thousands of years until finally it forms the Om. So Om is the vibration of consciousness that produced a cosmic sound, back in the process of creation, before creation was around to have physical hearing apparatuses known as ears to hear with, consciousness had cosmic hearing capacity, and created a cosmic sound, that originally was just an almost imperceptible vibration, within static consciousness.

Om is one of the names of God, but it is God without any shape or form, the formless sound, and it is called the pranava, the original vibration.

Shiva: Nirguna and Saguna: Form and the Formless

Shivaya is just a fancy way of saying Shiva, and who is Shiva? Shiva and Shakti are two major figures in Tantra. Shiva is consciousness, and Shakti is energy or power. Together they unite in a cosmic dance that brings the phenomenal world into being, and this energetic dance, which is considered to manifest the highest perfection of the most pure light, is also considered to be our true core identity: it is spanda.

The formless aspect of the deity is called nirguna and is generally considered to be vast and beyond our comprehension, while the aspect that has form is called saguna and portrays Lord Shiva in the form of a man. There is much to explore in saguna Shiva – many images and rich symbolism are revealed in the visual forms of Lord Shiva.

There are also many mantras to both Shiva and Shakti. One beautiful mantra to Lord Shiva is called Shiva Dhyanam which means meditation on Shiva, and it also gives us images that relate to the saguna and nirguna aspects of Lord Shiva:

Oṁ sadā śivayā vidmahe sahaśrākṣāya dhīmahe tanno śambho pracodayāt

Which means

oṁ We meditate upon the Perfect, Full, Complete, Always Continuing, Consciousness of Infinite Goodness; contemplate He Whose Thousand Eyes see everywhere. May that Giver of Bliss grant us increase.

(p. 11, *Śiva Pūjā and Advanced Yajña* by Swami Satyananda Saraswati and Swami Vittalananda Saraswati)

Thus begins the much beloved Shiva Dhyanam, a sacred song to Lord Shiva that is traditionally sung/chanted at Maha Shivaratri. It is also chanted at some Shiva temples continuously. Shivaratri is a yearly festival in honor of Lord Shiva, which happens on the dark of the moon in February or March. Participants try to stay up all night chanting, praying, and worshipping, dancing and celebrating, to welcome the morning light. In effect, Shivaratri is about bringing light into darkness, and Lord Shiva, consciousness, is light.

Lord Shiva's skin is often depicted as blue – the color of the sky – and he blends in with the sky. He has a crescent moon in his hair, and he dances the tandava, the sacred dance of creation and destruction. On Maha Shivaratri, some like to dress up as Lord Shiva and paint their skin blue and act out the part where Lord Shiva dances the tandava with his partner Goddess Shakti. On this day; Lord Shiva is ritually offered milk, flavored with saffron and honey, to calm him from the venom he drank to save humanity. Drinking the venom caused his throat to turn blue, and is why he is often depicted with blue skin.

If Lord Shiva is blue as the sky, this may come as no surprise. In Sri Vijnana Bhairava Tantra, one of the meditations given is to meditate on the vast emptiness of the deep blue sky. If one meditates on the vast blue sky, gazing into it, one will have a vision of Lord Bhairava, a form of Lord Shiva.

While Shiva is often depicted as blue like the sky, he is also often depicted as white, representing the pure light of consciousness, and the pillar of light (Shiva lingam – mark of Lord Shiva). Shiva is often depicted as white also because he sometimes covers himself in ash when he haunts the cremation grounds.

Lord Shiva also has a special connection to the crown chakra, the energy center on the top of the head, since this is the place that Shiva or consciousness is said to rise to where it unites with Shakti or energy to create enlightenment. Actually Lord Shiva is also sometimes depicted as wearing a headpiece with the image of Shakti rising from his brow as that crown, over the top of his ample locks of long hair that are wound on top of his head. His Shakti is his crowning glory and without her, Shiva remains inert, until Kundalini Shakti rises up to the crown, uniting with Shiva in an explosion of metaphysical bliss.

At the top of the head, one finds the crown chakra or the sahasrara chakra as it is known in Sanskrit. The reason the crown chakra is called sahasrara, is that it is the chakra with one thousand petals. The thousand petals in the crown chakra, are like the thousand eyes of Lord Shiva mentioned in the first line of the Shiva Dhyanam, quoted at the start of this segment. In a very real sense, the thousand eyes of Lord Shiva can be seen as a reference to the expanded state of mind: the senses that can pick up on information on so many levels, in so many ways. One might say the thousand eyes of Lord Shiva are a reference to the thousand petals of the crown chakra, and represent spiritual sight or intuition that extends beyond ordinary senses into the metaphysical: the thousand eyes of Lord Shiva see "everywhere." So, too, our own inner nature, when awake and ignited with the fire of devotion and the light of consciousness, can sense and "see" and know in ways that sometimes evade our conscious mind.

In a way we could say that Shiva is God – the Supreme Being, consciousness and infinite light – and that's what he is. In the West we tend to think of God as a person, because that's what we are exposed to a lot with Christianity. Christianity has the person of God the Father and the person of Jesus. The Holy Spirit is more in the direction of the formless aspect of God but the Holy Spirit doesn't get a lot of press, and is believed to be the indwelling aspect of God who resides in the heart of Christians. In *Hall of Faith Classics Volume 1: The Person and Work of the Holy Spirit:*

As revealed in Scripture and in Personal Experience, author R. A. Torrey characterizes the Holy Spirit as a person who lives in the individual hearts of Christians. Hindus and Tantrics also often think of Lord Shiva as residing in our hearts.

In Tantra and Hinduism in general, there is always this play between the form of a deity (its image and likeness) and the formless aspect of God: the Ultimate which is beyond our comprehension. As pure consciousness, Shiva is the formless and the Ultimate – nirguna. He can also be thought of as God in his saguna aspect, wherein he is oft depicted as a man, seated in meditation, and is something that we can relate to, and symbolically represents real qualities of Lord Shiva.

If we can see with our eyes, then Absolute Consciousness must have the capacity for sight inherently, even without physical eyes, and the capacity for hearing inherently even without physical ears. How do we know this? We know this because that's what consciousness is and does: it sees and hears and senses and knows through what it perceives.

The nirguna aspect is the highest Shiva. He is God who is formless. Then the lower Shiva, the one who incarnates into the form of a man, who embodies himself incarnating as individual souls in humanity, he is the Shiva who has form. Saguna Shiva has form. Nirguna Shiva is beyond form. Saguna Shiva who has form, is depicted in the form of a man. He is oft depicted seated in meditation, covered in white ash, with little clothing, maybe just a tiger skin loincloth. Lord Shiva has the crescent moon in his hair, and even the Ganges River flows through his big head of wild curly and matted locks of hair. Lord Shiva is an ascetic or somebody who takes austerities in order to devote himself to spiritual development. He lives high up on Mount Kailasha where the Gods live, and meditates alone on the mountain with his eyes closed. He often defies convention and is seen wandering the graveyards, a very powerful and terrifying sort.

In fact, one form of Lord Shiva, known as Bhairava, who also has a whole Tantra devoted to him, (the *Sri Vijnana Bhairava Tantra*) symbolizes the soul's longing for God – as the lone wolf howls at the moon in the dark of the night, so the soul moans and longs for God in the dark night of the soul, and Bhairava is the embodiment of this quality of the soul longing for God and feeling that God is far off. Bhairava, a fierce form of the God of Destruction (Shiva is the God of Destruction), destroys evil spirits and gets rid of negative energy, and ignorance.

As far as Shiva being far away goes, we can perceive him in two ways: as one with our own soul; or as standing about two feet away.

Lord Shiva spends half his time as a married man, married to Goddess Parvati, with whom he has two children, Ganesh and Kartikeya.

Shiva is also often depicted as Shiva Nataraja or lord of the dance. In this form he is depicted dancing wildly, balancing on one foot, twirling, balancing all of creation as he dances.

Consciousness has for one thing everywhere, timelessly and atemporally, eyes and ears. Yes it's true that in the beginning when the first sound Om emanated from the movement of energy in consciousness, there were no physical ears and no physical eyes but the assumption is here made, according to Tantra, that consciousness has the capacity of sight and hearing and experiences the Om in its own cosmic way. If ultimate consciousness is holding our reality in being, it is conscious and aware at every point in creation. It hears like cosmic consciousness, not a cacophony of sounds, but all sounds happening in the world distinctly. Because it is cosmic consciousness, it has the power to do this, and this sort of thing is in part what makes the Ultimate beyond our ability to comprehend, and why we need to create saguna Shiva, a God who is like a person, that we can relate to, a Lord Shiva who is seated in meditation, a God who has human qualities, who wants us to evolve, who knows when we meditate, who sees us with his eyes, who hears us with his ears, who knows us with his mind, and who cares about our evolution with his heart.

In fact, what Lord Shiva wants is for us to know ourselves. Lord Shiva wants us to come to know our own inner self as consciousness. We are created with a spiritual self or soul that has the capacity for enlightenment, so this capacity is built into our very nature by God: why wouldn't God know and care about our evolution if we are created by God to evolve in this way? When we can connect with Lord Shiva that is latent within us, we realize we are one with God – one with the cosmic consciousness that is veiled within us, and we have accomplished what we are here for. We are here to learn and grow inwardly and to become aware of our full potential, and to learn that we are made of the same stuff as Shiva and Shakti united, or energy, consciousness and being. We are a microcosm of the macrocosm, a hologram, a chip off the old block. We are the same stuff as the Divine Ultimate, at our root, eternal and without beginning or end.

Lord Shiva – consciousness – is the purest light that is brighter than the brightest sun. Lord Shiva is the light. Shakti or energy moves and gives flashes of light in consciousness. Shakti is light.

When we meditate by chanting Om Namah Shivaya, we are using the name of Lord Shiva, and vibrating with his same vibration. We should find within us a reverence for God, or if you prefer to think in terms of the vastness of the Ultimate, have awe and reverence for that, because it is bigger than us. If consciousness is holding creation in being, it is not our individual consciousness that is doing so. It is a vaster cosmic consciousness that is so vast we cannot even begin to comprehend it. So we should have an attitude of respect when chanting mantras.

The word "namah" in the mantra is all about respect, and that's what it means: I bow to you, I acknowledge your presence in my life.

The mantra is vibrations and those vibrations are sacred: in fact, according to Tantra, the vibrations themselves are said to be the vibrations of Lord Shiva himself. When consciousness vibrates with energy, that is what it's all about, and we can experience that and become one with the source of the All, which is consciousness and energy. We can begin to move beyond discursive thinking, at a very basic level, and move closer to pure consciousness. Everything about it is sacred.

Any mantra really is all about the vibrations. It's also about what it means at the level where we reflect on it as dhyana or contemplation. But the purpose of mantras is to bring us to that level where we are experiencing the vibrations on the inner level.

There are various ways to experience the vibrations. On the one hand, as has been mentioned, we can physically feel them in our physical body with our physical senses. And we can begin to become sensitive to the vibrations of the mantras on subtler levels as well, within our chakras and our energy body. We don't have to be conscious of all this happening, but we can just know it is happening in the background, and that this is what the mantra japa is all about.

Tantric Japa Yoga is all about the vibrations. We vibrate with the mantra and the mantra is the vibrations of the deity and we become one with the deity. Every mantra that is for a specific deity vibrates with the same energy as that deity itself. Truly the deity began as a state of mind in our contemplation of creation – the saguna aspect of the deity is a creation of our imagination. Inwardly we become one with the vibration, that aspect of the Ultimate which has everything in it. By chanting the mantra and making the vibrations, we become of one vibration with Lord Shiva, or one with God, and can experience expanded states that give us a feeling of what the vast expanded consciousness of Lord Shiva might be like.

In Tantra, Lord Shiva is real, but in truth he is formless, beyond our conception, so the forms of Shiva are created by our imagination as we contemplate the qualities of absolute consciousness. We imagine him in ways that make sense, that come from our own sense of what it is like to experience the world as consciousness: seeing with our eyes, hearing with our ears, sensing with our senses and all the information feeding our consciousness, so we have things to be conscious of.

The Ultimate has everything in it and nothing would exist if it weren't in the Ultimate: so every person, every plant, rock, and animal, and every vibration in the cosmos is all part of the Ultimate, and is made of the same consciousness, energy and being as the Absolute.

When we tune inwardly, through vibration, to our innermost self, one of the things that happens is that the discursive or the thinking mind slows down, or takes a break, and we find peace. In our active waking states as soon as we are awake we have to make choices and our consciousness clenches with the effort we make as we move through our days. It takes a conscious effort to refocus ourselves for meditation, to turn the attention within and stop doing, stop thinking, stop watching tv, or listening to music, and stop focusing the attention outward, and start to bring the attention within. As the mind stills, we become more aware of ourselves as pure consciousness – the clenching of consciousness around the need to decide relaxes as it does in deep sleep.

Om Namah Shivaya and the Five Elements

We can break Om Namah Shivaya down into parts. Om is Om, the transcendental element. Na represents earth. Ma represents water. Shi is fire. Va is air. And Ya represents sky or ether. So when we chant Om Namah Shivaya it vibrates all the pancha maha bhutas, or all five elements within us and is said to purify the elements within us.

Om Namah Shivaya is a powerful mantra that can still the mind, and wash out all the old samskaras, bringing fresh energy and a clear mind. Ultimately it can lead one to liberation, which is the final realization of the inner self.

I think in the start of my practice I didn't realize that in Tantra, Shiva is God. I abstracted Shiva as consciousness and I didn't make the connection that the vast consciousness is God, like the God whom we often envision as a person. Shiva is consciousness and Divine Mother is vibration of consciousness or energy and motion of consciousness. The two are inseparable and Shiva exists in many various states from the pure inert state to the state where he comes down and exists all the way in humans. He comes down like God –

as consciousness, light and being – lives in our heart, yet he is the vastness of consciousness and is quantum – infinitely small yet infinitely vast. Our world is quantum and in quantum science consciousness comes first. In Tantra, consciousness comes first and it is God.

Om Namah Shivaya: TJY Assignment #1

Shajesh gave me Om Namah Shivaya, Phase One, Tantric Japa Yoga. I was thrilled and ready to get started. At that time I didn't realize the bit about consciousness being God, and I just had this westerners notion of consciousness as a vast abstract concept, not consciousness as Being, that has sight, hearing, presence, and that is aware of all things at all times, not just vaguely as if sensing a cacophony of sounds, but infinitely specific to all points and locations. I just thought flatly of consciousness as being awareness – as if it was all about the awareness inside my own head (and it is about all that too). I didn't realize Shiva is God. I knew he is Lord Shiva and that he sits in meditation, covered in white ash, like a meditating ascetic, but I thought that was symbolic. And it *is* symbolic. Lord Shiva as a man is a covering for the sake of storytelling in the human realm – for teaching and using what we can relate to, to create a feeling of connection to divinity. Still, I was falling prey to the erroneous notion that other peoples' religions are myths, which implies "not true." Though we tend to assume religion we are raised with is true. I was thinking, "oh, this consciousness is a scientific thing. Many tantric traditions believe that Lord Shiva is the Supreme Being, and/or that the Divine Mother is the Supreme Being. It is believed that this Supreme Being created us so that we will evolve spiritually and therefore, naturally cares about our spiritual growth. And when we begin to chant daily to Lord Shiva, over time he will become real to us.

Saguna Shiva has three eyes, just like we do. We are like Lord Shiva in that way: we have two physical eyes and one third-eye or spiritual eye for seeing into our inner realities. Or rather, we have three eyes like Shiva, or the ability to see inner, subjective and subtle realities, as well as outer, objective realities.

One of the things that we are supposed to do in Phase One of Tantric Japa Yoga is to focus on the third-eye, and notice the vibration there, as well as anywhere else it may occur in our bodies

Focusing on the third-eye (the space between the eyebrows in the center of the forehead), with the eyes closed, is in itself a form of meditation. When we close our eyes and see the dark blank space before our mind's eye, that space is called chidakasha, and gazing there is called chidakasha dharana. Dharana is a form of concentration. While we are watching the flow of the mind, we are doing what is called antar mouna. And, while we contemplate the meaning of the mantra, we are doing dhyana, another form of meditation that entails contemplating prayer or spiritual song or verse. Meanwhile, we are chanting the mantra Om Namah Shivaya, and really we are supposed to just chant, while gazing into the third-eye and noticing any vibration we may feel there (or any vibration we may feel anywhere else in the body).

When I say we are supposed to "just chant" Om Namah Shivaya, I mean just that. We just have to chant and continue to repeat the mantra over and over and keep the focus on the mantra, on the sounds made by the words and really, most of all, on the vibrations. In Tantra we focus on the vibrations. We don't have to meditate on the meaning of Lord Shiva. On the other hand, if we do meditate on the meaning of Lord Shiva while we are chanting, it is just adding a layer to your meditation, because otherwise the mind may be wandering. Also, if we know anything about Lord Shiva, images and impressions of Lord Shiva and or realities related to Lord Shiva, such as expanded states of consciousness, may arise out of the teeming activity of the mind. And we just keep refocusing on chanting the mantra while gazing into the third-eye. Even if we just focus on chanting and not on the meaning of the mantra, the meaning is there in us if we know the meaning, so it is being activated in us on a subtle level, even if we are not actively thinking about it.

Chanting should focus the mind, and if we continue to focus on chanting, it will focus our mind. If we focus on the meaning of Om Namah Shivaya while we chant and feel the vibrations, it may help to keep the mind focused. If we have a very hard time staying focused in meditation, we could even imagine the words as we chant them spelled out before our mind's eye in chidakasha, the blank space before the mind's eye, as we chant. We don't have to imagine the words, but if it helps us meditate and stay focused that is what it's all about.

It's all about bringing the attention within and stilling the discursive mind. But the discursive mind has its own momentum, its own gravity, its own pull, and sometimes it's hard to get the discursive mind to settle down. We do so by coaxing the mind with practices, rather than trying to force the mind, so even if we are just chanting the mantra and bursts of thought keep erupting into our japa, we keep our mind focused on repeating the mantra, gently turning our mind away from thoughts, back to the mantra. We let go of any thoughts that erupt, and keep bringing our focus back to our mantra and the vibrations, as we gaze into the third-eye. Focusing attention here has the power to activate the third-eye. So we just keep chanting and maintain the focus of our meditation.

Chanting "Om Namah Shivaya" is like a song that sooths the soul.

You can feel the vibrations as you chant on day one and you can focus on making beautiful vibrations. You will have a new mantra in your toolbox and you can chant it anytime you like. It is yours.

*** Practice Notes***

I recommend making note cards for your practice. Write instructions and all the mantras you will need to chant on note cards and keep them with you when you chant while you are learning the mantras and practices.

This will be worth the time you invest at the start, because it will make it easier to find your way through the practices as you practice.

***

There are always going to be distractions and we should not say or expect that we will meditate without distraction. Rather, if you want to set an intention, say that you will continue to bring your mind back to chanting. When we sit for meditation with minimized external distractions, in private, we can go deep into meditation. We can also have beautiful experiences as we chant while we go about our day and tune out distractions while we continue to bring our attention back to the mantra. Distractions are always going to be there: it's how we deal with them that's important.

***

Start simple and build. You can see that from Om Namah Shivaya we go on to Gayatri, another basic and a staple in Hinduism and Tantra, a mantra that many people know, that is the essence of the Vedas. Chanting Om Gayatri Om and keeping the attention at the chakras, as instructed in Phase Two of Tantric Japa Yoga, is clearly more complex than simply chanting Om Namah Shivaya. And still, you get to chant Om Namah Shivaya and add Gayatri to it. So the endurance for more self-discipline is being stretched and the tapas is increasing gradually as the difficulty increases. It's a very good program, and even if you follow the program you can take your time. You can chant 45 days and move on or just keep chanting Phase Two for a whole year, then when you are ready, try the next phase. But there is never any opportunity to get bored on your journey.

You may find that after 45 days of practice, the mind may start to wander, because you are starting to know it better and don't have to concentrate so hard to get it right. You have to simply concentrate on your practice and that is your discipline. Then, when you get a new assignment, you have to concentrate harder again because it is all new and you have to learn it. And after 45 days has passed, by that time you will find the assignment too easy and you may find your mind starts to wander. Then you will have a new assignment to learn and this will draw your mind deeper into the practice as well as into the unfolding story that is creating a big picture over time.

Personally, I have tried to stay with the 45 days of practice, then move on to the next phase as advised by my guru, Shajesh. However, sometimes I did miss days, and when I miss days, I do not count those days. I move the count to the next day of practice and pick it up there, so that

45 days is not half gone by without practice, but 45 actual days of practice.

***

Resist the temptation to share too much with others about your practice. They may not appreciate it like you do, and there is something to be said for keeping privacy. Even if somebody knows you, and you are practicing in the home and they support you, it may be best to limit what you share. Keep your meditation in your own mental realms. Sure, if you lose focus or balance due to negative energy affecting you, you can regain your focus, but little disturbances to the energy and flow of practice are irritants one can do one's best to avoid, and deal with them, learn something, and move on if it happens.

***

When chanting a mantra for a specific number of repetitions, you can use a mala of 108 beads, rolling the thumb over one bead at a time as you go, or use the fingers to count, touching the tip of the thumb to tips and knuckles of fingers as you go. When using a mala, do not count the end bead, but return and count back around the other way when you reach the end bead, which is called the guru bead.

Now let's learn Phase One Tantric Japa Yoga:

Phase One Tantric Japa Yoga:

Om Namah Shivaya:

Sit in sukhasana, a comfortable seated position, on a flat surface, with legs crossed. It's best to have a lift under the hips when sitting for meditation, to encourage a straight spine, and for blood flow to the legs.

Energy breathing:

Do kapalbathi pranayama for three, one-minute rounds, as described below:

Kapalbathi Pranayama:

With eyes closed, breathe through the tip of the nose.

As you inhale, the belly should push out naturally.

On the exhale, the belly button should push toward the spine forcefully on a quick burst of exhale.

Let the inhale come in naturally. Do not inhale in a prolonged way, but briefly, naturally.

The exhale is always forceful, with belly pumping toward spine.

Again, inhale; this pushes the belly out in a relaxed and brief way.

Continue breathing in this way, pumping the belly in on the exhale and relaxing it out on the inhale,

Continue for one minute.

After one minute of kapalbhati breathing, pause for a little while, breathing peacefully and naturally with the eyes closed, and experience samadhi, the peaceful feeling you get after doing the breathing.

Mantra meditation:

As you chant, concentrate on the vibration of the mantra in ajna (the brow chakra); and wherever else you feel it in the body. Gaze inwardly, focusing on the third-eye – the space between the eyebrows in the center of the forehead. The third-eye is located in chidakasha, the blank space before the mind's eye:

Chant:

Om Namah Shivaya

20 minutes

Relax, and practice samadhi, feeling the peaceful feelings for a few minutes. If you have a teacher, you can feel the blessings from your teacher. Otherwise, practice samadhi.

Say:

Om Shanti Shanti Shanti

After 45 days of practice, continue on to TJY Phase Two.

Note

Dakshina is the old way of paying one's guru and of showing respect and gratitude. The student determines how much dakshina to give, putting coins in a jar after each meditation practice as given by the guru. There is no set price. The guru gives the practices freely to the student and the student gives the Dakshina freely to the guru.

***

Now you have been given Phase One of Tantric Japa Yoga, and this much, if you continue to do it beyond the first forty five days, over time, can bring you to liberation, otherwise known as moksha. If you want to continue with Tantric Japa Yoga, practice Phase One for 45 days, then move on to Phase Two.

Mantra Japa and Prayer

Do we ever really get the feeling that consciousness is God, that energy is Goddess, and that together they are Brahman? That we can pray to them? Petition them? That they are present and listening, seeing and active in our lives guiding us along when they see us making efforts to evolve ourselves?

If you want to use chanting outside your regular practice times, for prayer purposes, you can take a few moments to set sankalpa or intention for your meditation: simply bring your palms together in prayer position in front of the heart chakra (called anjali mudra), then, in a few sentences, let Shiva know why you are chanting now. As I could say this morning "I am worried about xy&z and pray all turns out well, therefore I dedicate my chanting to this."

As you begin to chant it becomes like a wordless prayer of the heart: all the feelings from the heart go out inexplicably on the vibrations as the soul sings.

Indeed, in Tantra, the heart is the seat of the mind. The heart is called hridaya. In referring to the heart we are referring to the heart chakra. In fact the name for the heart chakra, (not the physical heart), is anahata, which means "unstruck sound." Sound that is produced by our vocal cords or other apparatuses is made by striking in a way so as to cause sound waves that travel through space to an ear apparatus so it can be heard. But cosmic sound is beyond the need for such apparatuses. And as we chant, on the cosmic level, the sound of the mantras are cleansing our samskaras (the patterns set down by past stress and trauma of the soul) and laying down new ones so we can move forward renewed and refreshed. So, if it is our heart's desire, we can use chanting as an opportunity for prayer. But this is not the same thing as doing discursive prayer.

Chapter Eight:
Lord Shiva the Ascetic

Lord Shiva is the perfect archetype of the perfect sadhaka. A sadhaka is a person who does spiritual practice and aspires to achieve moksha or liberation. In fact, Lord Shiva is one with the Absolute and is often considered to be the Ultimate Reality or Supreme Being in Tantra. So, he represents the final goal of the tantric sadhaka.

Lord Shiva is also the first guru. A guru is a spiritual teacher who belongs to a lineage of teachers, who transmits the oral tradition, or passes along the lineage teachings to the aspirant. Shiva first taught his wife Parvati, then she taught what he taught her to the rishis and seers, so he was also the first guru. The rishis then transmitted what they learned to humanity. Shiva is also the first yogi, and dances the tandava, balanced on one foot, as he balances creation.

Lord Shiva is a unique character archetype for us in the West. We do not have such a character as Lord Shiva. In the West we have a lot of Christianity so most are at least somewhat familiar with the archetype of Lord Jesus, who was not a loner. On the one hand there are times when he did go away in private to pray, such as when he spent 40 days in the desert after being baptized by the apostle John. But these times in Jesus life do not archetypally define who he is. Jesus is seen more as a teacher among crowds. While his 40 days in the desert do reflect something of a spiritual quest, it is a lone, isolated incident that merely defines his initiation into the call. When he comes back from the desert, he is Lord Jesus, and he teaches the multitudes. The only other time we ever see him alone, is in the Garden of Gethsemane. Yes this is one of the archetypes of Jesus, and we can often see him on pictures or book marks painted in this scene, where he is seated with hands folded in prayer, praying to the light on high that is shining down from the clouds up in heaven, praying to God. This is Jesus the son of God talking to his father on high in heaven, looking for solace.

Lord Shiva sits in meditation, his eyes closed, deep in samadhi, in perfect union with the cosmic consciousness that he himself also represents, perfectly one with all, attained – the Ultimate itself. He sits and meditates in a deep state of absorption. He is the ascetic in this scene, with no needs. Shiva has no needs because he contains everything within him, so in this state he is ascetic, seated alone on the mountain, Mount Kailash where the Gods live, and is one with the Ultimate, which he is.

He represents our innermost self, and it is said that when we achieve moksha, the worldly desires will hold no more sway over us. We will continue to go through our lives but we won't be dominated by our desires. Instead, we will be one with cosmic consciousness just like Lord Shiva when he is in meditation, with the same powers of consciousness within our own sphere of limited influence. Lord Shiva indeed lives in the heart of the aspirant.

Christianity has the Holy Spirit and the Holy Spirit is also a person who lives in the heart, at least according to R.A. Torrey, in Hall of Faith Classics Volume 1: The Person and Work of the Holy Spirit. Having awareness of the deity in our hearts gives us a kind of special power. It sets up a dialectic with the inner spirit and gives us a sense of inner presence. When we have attained moksha, we merge with this sense of inner presence, become one with it and then we find ourselves in what is called the non-dual state. And this non-dual state is what Lord Shiva represents when he is depicted seated in meditation with his eyes closed. The non-dual state means that we experience ourselves as one with that inner consciousness which is also one with the Absolute.

"Namaste" is a popular Hindu greeting often heard in yoga classes, which very simply means "I bow to you." But, more elaborately it means and has been said to express: "I honor the place in you where the entire universe dwells. When you are in that place in you, and I am in that place in me, we are one." This is what Lord Shiva represents.

Lord Shiva is the one without a second. He is one with all creation. When he is seated in meditation on Mount Kailash he is consciousness in our heart.

Lord Shiva has the Ganges River running through his hair, which shows us how vast he is. Ganges River is depicted as a Goddess, so he has the divine feminine running through his big head of wild hair. Ganges is also a place people go to in pilgrimage for reconnecting with the divine, for spiritual blessing and salvation.

Shiva also has the moon in his hair, which shows his ability to balance emotional states, which is something we too should be able to do.

Shiva is often depicted as being covered in white ash, which is a symbol of the cremation ground he is sometimes said to haunt. Those who are associated with the cremation ground are not a part of mainstream society. The cremation ground symbolizes detachment from the cycles of life and death. Again, when we reach awakening, enlightenment, or moksha, we are said to be no more bound by the cycles of rebirth and death, and merge with universal consciousness.

This is what Shiva as guru demonstrates for us. And we have no archetype for this in the West – no archetype of a loner who sits in endless meditation detached from it all. In the West we have the archetype of worldly success – those who succeed in worldly society tend to be our role models. We have the archetypes of teachers and doctors and lawyers and all sorts of archetypes of people who participate in the worldly social realm. And it's all good.

From Christianity, which is prevalent in much of the western world, we do have the image of Jesus in the Garden of Gethsemane praying. And, I have seen that when in the middle of a football game, something happens, and a member of the team is seriously injured, the rest of the team all drop down on one knee in a stance of prayer, to align with the divine will in the sincere hopes their teammate will live. So on a deep level, that archetype of Jesus praying is out there, in western society. We know that at least in those rare moments, such as for Jesus when he knew he was about to be sacrificed to the cross, we can call on God. Jesus knew this and was in emotional crisis, praying to God to be spared. "Oh father if it be possible take this cup from me" and yet, Jesus being son of God, God did not take that cup from him and Jesus proved his mastery over death and his lordship when he resurrected. But as for Jesus praying. We have him praying only on special occasions like at the last supper or in a crisis, like impending crucifixion. So, we have Jesus praying at the last supper and what do we see in the West? We get people like the father of the bride making speeches at weddings, which aren't the last supper in reality but are important occasions where someone assume the temporary role of the head of the group and speaks profoundly or sometimes says prayers. And it's all good.

But we do not have the archetype of somebody who makes the private time and space on a regular basis for meditation. Meditation is becoming more popular. Now, many meditate. Well, let's put that in numbers. According to the National Health Interview Survey, 17.3% of adults practiced meditation in the USA in 2022, more than double from 2002. Meditation is becoming more popular and yet it is still not a huge percentage of people in the West who meditate.

Now, consider that according to a 2021 Pew Research Center Study, roughly half of adults in India, or 48%, practice meditation weekly, while 32% practice daily.

What kind of different society would we have if we had the archetype of Lord Shiva looming over us in big life-size statues, and what if 47% of Americans meditated? What if we cared about our inner world? What if we didn't feel like it was some negative stigma to go to therapy and do self-study? And what if we didn't feel we have to hide any signs of spiritual experience, fearing judgement? What if we realized that good therapy is a part of svadhyaya or self-study and we became more self-aware? What if we meditated regularly and even experienced kundalini energy?

Many people are activating prana in meditation. Many people have activated kundalini and experience it regularly in meditation. It may be a small percentage but the numbers are growing. Those who experience the full awakening, it is said, are somewhat rare. But just having kundalini active in our system is a sign we are spiritually evolving and are on the path. Maybe in this life time or in the next we will experience the full deal.

Personally, I am taking my time.

One day, in meditation, I had an experience of light shooting up into my head in the front part of my brain, and I told Shajesh about it and he told me "Don't try to make it happen. Just meditate"

I have gotten the impression after reading widely, that people who try too hard to make it happen, try against all odds, are determined and do everything they can just with the goal of awakening kundalini, sometimes succeed and end up awakening it very suddenly, in a strong way; still some who try very hard, do not achieve in activating kundalini anyways by their intense efforts; so kundalini has a mind of her own and cannot be forced. The real goal is not to have dramatic experiences, but to learn and grow, and experience expanded states of consciousness, more mental clarity and energy, and the host of benefits that can come from regular meditation.

What is important is the transformation of consciousness and this is what Shiva represents. That we should transform our consciousness through meditation and tuning in to our inner world. This can take time and that is okay.

On the other hand, sitting in meditation is only half the story about Lord Shiva. When he comes down from Mount Kailash he returns to being married to Parvati, and has two children. Then he partakes of the affairs of the world. So also in this he is a good archetype for us, because we can't sit in meditation forever: we have to come out of meditation and take care of our worldly duties – our worldly dharma. Tantra says we can live our lives and still be on the path to moksha.

Even if we are jivamukti, and achieve moksha in this life and are liberated in our bodies, we still will have to get up in the morning and wash the dishes and fix ourselves something to eat, to take care of our bodies and interact with people in the world.

We get to know Lord Shiva by chanting his mantras and praying to him. This is how we set up the dialectic. It helps us process our experience to have that sounding board – that conceptual other in the heart, who our hearts' longings, prayers, and concerns go out to, and our gratitude when things go right. Over time this cultivates our relationship with Lord Shiva or whatever deity we are praying to, just like talking to a friend would cultivate the relationship with that friend.

Chapter Nine:
TJY Phase Two:
Om-Gayatri-Om

Om, Bhur Bhuva Swah,

Tat Savitur Varenyam,

Bargo Devasya Dhimahi

Diyo yo nah prachodayat.

Gayatri Mantra

The Gayatri Mantra is an ancient hymn from the Rig Veda. The Rig Veda is one of four Vedas or sacred scriptures which are believed in Hinduism to be divinely inspired; the Rig Veda is the oldest and the largest of the Vedas and is the oldest literature of Hinduism.

The Gayatri Mantra is called Gayatri because that is the meter it is written in. Gayatri is a solar goddess. The mantra, which is dedicated to Goddess Gayatri, also features the solar deity Savitur. Savitur is the sun at the precise moment before sunrise, when the golden aura of the sun can be seen preceding the sun on the eastern horizon, and begins to lighten the sky, bringing an end to the darkness of night. During the daytime, the sun is called Surya, and is Surya until the sun sets again in the evening. Surya is not involved in the Gayatri Mantra.

The Gayatri mantra is an ancient hymn or prayer for enlightenment, and it is said to be the essence of the Vedas. The Gayatri Mantra tells a story, and this story in a nutshell really sums up the message in the Vedas. The Vedas are the ancient Hindu scriptures that are passed down by divine revelation. The Vedas explain much about humanity's desire to evolve as embodiments of consciousness and act as a spiritual guide.

Om, as the sacred original vibration, is to be at the start of all mantras, and so we see it at the start of Gayatri Mantra. Also, the reading of the Vedas is to be preceded by Om and followed by Om.

The first line of Gayatri Mantra is a creation story. It starts with Om. We already know that Om is the original vibration. All the other sounds of the Sanskrit alphabet evolve out of Om, and each one does a special job by representing a unique aspect in the process of creation of the universe out of consciousness and energy. Eventually out of some of the sounds, matter begins to form, and the material world is created. Om is a crucial point in the beginning of creation because it is the original vibration, or the original movement of energy in consciousness. The original wave of self-awareness and self-reflection arose out of this primal consciousness and Om is the original sound that emanated from the cosmic consciousness, when a little spuratta of light energy erupted in consciousness, and out of the cosmic stillness and out of the cosmic silence, energy and consciousness stirred, and there was spanda, or vibration, in consciousness, and slowly, over thousands of years, the process of creation started from very subtle elements until the material world was formed. Om is truly the formless, beyond conception, before any name. Om is just a vibration, but a vibration that was so cosmic, it was the vibration of energy in consciousness, and things began to move in the process of creation of matter from consciousness, which reflects the laws of quantum physics, which tell us that consciousness precedes matter.

In the West, most scientists still believe that consciousness is produced by matter, by the brain. According to a National Institute of Health ("*Carl Gustav Jung, Quantum Physics, and the Spiritual Mind: A Mystical Vision of the Twenty-first Century.*" Diogo Valadus Ponte & Lother Schaefer, 2013, (Creative Commons) https://pmc.ncbi.nlm.nih.gov/articles/PMC4217602)

> "Quantum physics is more than physics: it is a new form of mysticism, which suggests the inter-connectedness of all things and beings and the connection of our minds with a cosmic mind."

Om is the first word of the Gayatri Mantra. Om – the cosmic vibration, the pranava, the beginning of everything, that almost moment when creation was about to express itself out of the bowels of consciousness and energy.

Om.

Bhur Bhuva Swah, the next words in the Gayatri mantra after Om, are the triple worlds that go out from the Om vibration.

Bhur is the earth;

Bhuva is beyond the earth our solar system;

Swah is the entire universe.

And so creation happened. There was a vibration in consciousness and Om emanated. Out of Om eventually matter evolved and things started being created, resulting finally in the three worlds mentioned in the Gayatri Mantra.

From our perspective as human beings, earth is first in proximity and first in our field of awareness. It is the earth beneath our feet, our grounding, our home. Next from our perspective we see the ever expanding orb of God's creation, our solar system, consisting of more planets still and a sun, and finally the entire universe, filled with many galaxies.

Tat Savitur Varenyam

From our perspective on the earth, amid the universal darkness, we see Savitur, the first glow of the predawn sun, on our horizon – foreshadowing the rising of the sun, and signaling the end of night.

Bargo Devasya Dhimahi

How specific this is to us: the sun lights our world! If not for the sun, we would not be here. How poignant that there is this sun about to rise on the eastern horizon and it is Savitur the delightful, predawn sun, the bright golden glow that begins to illuminate the darkness. This is very personal. This is for us. This sustains us and warms our world. This sparks every life form into being. This light is the symbol of the divine one. The sun is said to be Brahman. Brahman is said to be light. Shiva is said to be light, Shakti is light. All the devs and devas are lights – are just one more ray of the infinite divine light.

Diyo yo nah Prachodayat

Then, as this orb of light appears on our horizon, at the brink of dawning in our world, we pray in that moment for enlightenment. That maybe this God, this being of light, who placed the sun in the sky for our benefit, who created us as spiritual and conscious beings with the capacity for enlightenment, would come into our meditation and enlighten us.

This is our way back to the source through our own within, through our own self-awareness, through finding the stillness within and within that stillness becoming aware of the sun on our inner horizon.

So the prayer says, let us meditate on this God who created the universe, who put this delightful light of the predawn sun, on our horizon. May this one bring the divine light also into our own within.

It is very poetic. The polytheism of Hinduism and Tantra is so poetic and there is so much beauty and freedom in it. And so many ways to talk about and think about God. The Gayatri Mantra is one of those ways and it is a very important mantra in Hinduism. Boys and girls are given Gayatri Mantra initiation in Hinduism so they will have this mantra through the teen years, and for their whole lives. Gayatri Mantra is also important in Tantric Japa Yoga. Gayatri Mantra is for everyone.

The Gayatri Mantra is a mantra one can chant that will serve for one's whole life. One does not have to get it from a guru, though a guru can give you a way to chant the mantra. Otherwise, all you have to do is just chant the mantra. In Tantric Japa Yoga, Phase Two, there is a special tantric way to chant the Gayatri Mantra – a special formula for success.

Also, in addition to chanting the assigned mantras, we will make use of Guru Mantra. If you have a guru and your guru gives you their personal Guru Mantra, you can chant that, or if not, you can chant this Guru Mantra below:

Guru Mantra:

Guru Brahma, Guru Vishnu, Guru Devo Maheshwara. Guru Sakshat, Param Brahma, Tasmay Shree Gurave Namaha, Tasmay Shree Gurave Namaha, Tasmay Shree Gurave Namaha.

This prayer is acknowledging the original gurus: Brahma, Vishnu and Shiva (Maheshwara is another name for Shiva) which are a trinity in Hinduism. Brahma is the ultimate, the creator, Vishnu is the sustainer, and Shiva (Maheshwara) is the destroyer. One is acknowledging that these forces of the cosmos, these expressions of absolute consciousness, are the original guru. Guru sakshat param brahma says that the teachers are the ones who show us the way to Brahman, which is the Ultimate and also is our true innermost self. Tasmay shree gurave namah means we bow to the guru, who is the realized soul, the parabrahma. This means that the guru is Brahma, the guru is Shiva, the guru is Vishnu, meaning if one has an earthly guru, or considering also the inner guru, this guru is also God, is in essence the same energy as God – the same energy as Brahma, Shiva and Vishnu.

Lord Shiva is the original guru in Tantra. As God consciousness, Lord Shiva taught spiritual secrets to Parvati who then taught them to the rishis, who then in turn transmitted this knowledge to humanity.

Now let's learn Phase Two of Tantric Japa Yoga:

Tantric Japa Yoga, Phase Two: Om-Gayatri-Om:

For TJY Phase Two, there are three parts: morning, midday, and night-time practices. The morning and night-time practices are the same and are given first below, before the midday practice:

Morning and Night-time Practice:

To be done in the morning, when you wake up, ideally before you get up out of the bed, and in the evening before you go to sleep at night. Sit in the bed and chant:

Guru Mantra one time;

Om Nama Shivaya, 20 minutes;

Guru Mantra one time.

Midday Practice:

Sometime in the day after shower: wear comfortable clothing; sit in Sukhasana, a comfortable or easy sitting position. You can adapt this to suit your needs by sitting on a cushion with your legs crossed.

In general, it is advisable to sit on a cushion or folded blanket, so that your hips are slightly raised above the level of your knees. This promotes a straight spine.

Sit relaxed, but with your spine extending upward, slightly lowering your chin toward your chest.

Make sure you are well settled in this position.

Pranayama:

Before chanting do the following pranayama breathing practices:

kapalbhati pranayama, three, minute-long rounds, (instructions given in Phase One)

nadi shuddhi pranayama (also called Nadi Shodhana, or alternate nostril breathing)

5 minutes or 10 rounds

Nadi Shodhana/Nadi Shuddhi (Alternate Nostril Breathing):

To do alternate nostril breathing, take your right hand and place the fourth finger (ring finger) on the left nostril, and the thumb on the right nostril, while the middle finger can rest in the center of the forehead. You can use the thumb and the fourth finger, alternately, to press then release the nostrils by turns.

1st press thumb on the right nostril and leave left nostril open, while inhaling, slowly and deeply, through the left nostril.

2nd press the left nostril with the fourth finger and release the right nostril, while slowly and completely exhaling through the right nostril.

3rd pressing the left nostril with the fourth finger, and inhale through the right nostril, slowly and deeply.

4th press the thumb on the right nostril and release the fourth finger from the left nostril, while exhaling through the left nostril.

You have now completed one round of nadi shodhana.

Throughout the process, do not strain, but breathe comfortably.

Om-Gayatri-Om: Chanting:

Om is chanted before and after Gayatri Mantra. Om chanting is divided into two types: first, before Gayatri Mantra, Om is chanted with a long o and a short m – Ooooooooum; then, after Gayatri Mantra, Om is chanted with a short o and a long m – oummmmmmmm. In Sanskrit, the m on the end of mantras is intended to be vibrated; this means that we do not cut the sound of short but let the m vibration linger a little while. This vibrating m has a special role in Sanskrit due to the fact that it vibrates in the top of the head, in the sahasrara chakra. The o vibrates more in the chest.

Chant:

Oooooooum 108 times or 10 minutes.

While chanting, concentrate on anahata, the heart chakra, and imagine energy rising from root to heart as you chant. In Tantra, the goal is to raise kundalini from the base to the crown. As we chant and stimulate the vibration within us, we work on activating kundalini by chanting, and invite the energy to rise up through the sushumna (the central channel) to the various chakras, through our mental efforts, as we visualize.

Chant: Gayatri Mantra 108 times or 20 minutes:

Om Bhur Bhuvah Swaha
Tat Savitur Varenyam
Bhargo Devasya Dhimahi
Dhi Yo Yo Nah Prachodayat.

While chanting, concentrate on ajna (the brow chakra), and imagine energy rising from heart to brow.

Chant:

Oummmmmmm 108 times or10 minutes.

While chanting, concentrate on sahasrara (the crown chakra). Imagine energy rising from brow to crown.

Om Namah Shivaya Chanting:

Chant:

Guru Mantra one time.

Chant:

Om Nama Shivaya 5 minutes or 108 times.

Chant:

Guru mantra one time.

Practice Samadhi

End with Om Shanti, Shanti, Shanti:

Shanti means peace in the otherworldly sense – not peace as this world gives, but a spiritual peace. When we say shanti, we say it three times: the first time is for ourselves; the second time is for somebody else; and, the third time is for everyone – the whole world.

Chant:

Om Shanti Shanti Shanti

This concludes Phase Two of Tantric Japa Yoga.
Practice for 45 days. Then, if you wish to continue on to TJY Phase Three, you may get the assignment from the guru.

Comments on Nadi Shodhana

In a way, nadi shodhana is like rubbing sticks together to try to make a fire. The breath massages the ida and pingala nadis by turn, with the inhale and the exhale, stimulating the energy in the hopes of igniting the energy to travel through the central channel up sushumna nadi. Another way to say this, is that nadi shodhana is one more way of stimulating prana in the body in hopes of eventually stimulating kundalini which lies coiled at the base of the spine and then when activated rises through sushumna to the crown chakra, creating enlightenment.

Nadi shodhana is a very balancing pranayama. It helps balance the energies between the right and left hemisphere of the brain. It is also calming to the nervous system and can help alleviate stress.

As you practice nadi shodhana, if you wish to bring more mental stimulation to the practice, you can add counting the breath, and counting evenly be sure to inhale for as long as you exhale, or you can inhale and chant Om mentally on an inhale and on an exhale chant Om again, silently. As you get better at comfortably increasing the duration of the inhale and the exhale, you can add chanting silently of Gayatri Mantra: chant the entire Gayatri Mantra on one inhale, silently in the mind, and then again on the exhale. This is a more advanced practice and you should stay with practicing nadi shodhana as it is for the 45 day duration of Phase Two, until the practice becomes natural to you, and then you can try to complicate it for yourself when you feel ready.

If your guru gives you an assignment, do it as it is given. If you are advancing by yourself and continue on beyond the 45 days, you can evolve the pranayama as feels appropriate to you.

If you want to achieve any new habit or pattern in your life, any new goal, it's more certain you will succeed if you choose a smaller goal to start with, and then having achieved the smaller goal, you can set additional smaller goals beyond that, to keep the progress going. Tantric Japa Yoga works in this way, starting with the simplest assignment, and assignments increasing in difficulty with each phase. As the complexity of the assignments evolves, so with it evolves the knowledge that one is opening to and learning about tantric spirituality.

Having said that, I might as well add now, that learning advances us on our path spiritually, too. It is another dimension of our overall evolution. Education is part of it. Having an active mental life and learning things is part of being fully alive and experiencing life to our maximum potential. Practices complement one another. Pranayama and mantra japa complement one another. Having a physical yoga asana practice complements these as well. Following our dharma or taking care of our responsibilities in life complements the other aspects of our self as an ever unfolding process.

We are not static beings. We are in constant flux, motion and evolution. According to Tantra we are reborn again and again, living one lifetime after another, a process called reincarnation. We are evolving across lifetimes for thousands of years, learning through living this grand experiment. The tools we learn and the practices we do support us as we go through life. They help us make the most of our life by making the best of ourselves. Making use of spiritual practices can maximize our potential by refreshing our system, energizing, relaxing, balancing, stimulating, and more.

A few words on Phase Two: It is said that Om should precede and follow a reading of the Vedas, and the Gayatri Mantra is said to be the essence of the Vedas, so it is fitting to chant Om before and after chanting Gayatri Mantra. This is not the only way to chant Gayatri Mantra. It is the Tantric Japa Yoga way from the ancient tantric Aananda Nath lineage that I am studying. Shajesh has told me these practices have been passed down through the ages, and he has given me his Guru Mantra so that I may consider myself part of that ancient lineage.

Where I share additional information, these are things I have learned both through practice and study over the past ten years.

Gayatri Devotion and Kundalini

Gayatri Mantra mentions the creation. The three worlds mentioned at the start of the Gayatri Mantra and which emanate from the Om vibration, are called vyahritis or worlds and they are three in Gayatri Mantra and seven in other places. They are interpreted in various ways. I like the interpretation that says Bhur is the earth world, Bhuva is the solar system, and Swah is the universe beyond our solar system. Bhur, Bhuva, Svah, can also refer to the causal body, the gross body, and the subtle body that God has created. We are supposed to meditate on these three worlds which all emanate from the Om Vibration, and then the very next image is of tat savitur varenyam, bhargo devasya dhimahi: let us meditate on the delightful light of the predawn sun. Then the final line is the petition, asking that just as the delightful first rays of the predawn sun bring light to darkness in our outer world, so in the inner world we ask for enlightenment. We ask because it makes logical sense, that this Divine Being who created all our world and put the sun in our world to light our days, would want to light our hearts and minds as well.

It is said also in Hinduism that there is an inner sun, and that we are asking the inner sun to light our way. Or, some have said it is tejas, not the sun; or Agni is warming our consciousness making transformation possible. If the universe is frigid and frozen there is no life, no movement, no transformation. Warmth is needed for transformation and in our world that warmth comes from the sun.

Our inner sun is symbolized by agni, the inner fire in Ayurveda, which is our inner processes of transformation, such as digestion, where food is transformed into energy and waste in the body. Agni is also responsible for metabolizing thoughts and emotions, transforming them into useful information. Agni is expressed in all sorts of ways in our body. The sun is Brahman, which is absolute consciousness, and the sun is also consciousness with warmth. It is not frozen. It has warmth that triggers life processes in the world of biological organisms. For our minds it has the warmth that can trigger transformation of consciousness.

However there is another fire within us and that fire is tejas, which in Ayurveda, is the power that brings us light or inner radiance. It is also a spiritual glow, or a glowing warmth in the aura. Warmth is life. Life cannot live in a frozen state.

When we say the Gayatri Mantra, we are praying to the Brahman. The sun is also considered to be Brahman, technically everything in all of creation is Brahman. The sun is Brahman, so that means the sun is consciousness, energy, being and light, with warmth that can trigger transformation. Tejas, this light within us, is stimulated by chanting the Gayatri Mantra. Chanting the mantra requires effort. We make this effort, and it is like rubbing two sticks together to make a fire. Tapas is heat generated from spiritual practice, from the effort required. By disciplining ourselves with the practice, we create heat and that heat of transformation is what brings the glow of tejas. So, by chanting the Gayatri Mantra, indeed by our own efforts, we are increasing our spiritual glow. The spiritual glow of tejas lights our mind and our consciousness, like an inner sun: just as the sun also lights our outer world. Also, the heat created by the discipline of chanting the mantra over time – tapas – transforms our samskaras or inner conditioning, so that old conditioning is transformed into something new. Old karmas are transformed, opening the way for change.

Tapas, the heat created by one's disciplined practice, is also used in kundalini yoga. Clearing out the old karmas is the prerequisite for the kundalini to be activated and creates the ground work. You can make tapas by any disciplined practice. If the challenge is greater, the tapas created will be greater. The heat of the fire of transformation will burn hotter, and transformation may happen more quickly, but could also be explosive and hard to deal with when all one's inner baggage gets stirred up at once, very fast.

So it's always okay to slow your practice down if it feels too intense. If it creates too much resistance in you. Maybe you need to slow down and evolve at your own pace. You don't need to keep cranking it up, increasing the tapas to get the maximum transformation in the shortest amount of time. You can take your time. Meditate as much as feels comfortable to you. No effort will go to waste. Any amount of meditation is a good thing.

And it's not just chanting that creates heat of tapas. If you want to create more heat from more tapas, add more practices. Do pranayama breathing exercise(s) before your chanting.

Chapter Ten:
TJY Phases Three & Four:
Ganesh, Lakshmi, & Tarpanam

For Ganesh Tarpanam I used a large stainless-steel bowl, and I set a small brass statue of a Ganesh on a pedestal so that it was like he was floating on the surface of the water. I had to draw a yantra on the top of the water at the start. A yantra is a geometric design that represents the energy of the deity. Then with each line of mantra, I had to take my two hands together and scoop up some water, pouring it gracefully out over the statue of Ganesh.

I had fun bringing it all together so I could do Ganesh Tarpanam. I had to have a lift under my hips while I sat by the bowl. It's actually physically challenging. Not the sort of challenge that gives one a cardio workout or anything, but I remember struggling at times with feeling crampy in my legs. The practice took me forty five minutes to complete and I have circulation problems in the left leg from prior clotting, so it's hard for me to sit for too long. I also struggled a little while with one of my arms getting a nerve pain in it.

And just when I least expected it, determined to get it all right and "see what happens to me" (my reason for doing it all, to see what it's like to do it all, to see why people are doing it) – Just when I least expected it, I did start to experience some energy. I experienced some energy in the base chakra and I felt some energy in my frontal brow and I felt my words turn into the sounds of bells as they poured out from my lips over my fingertips with the water into the bowl, I had a sense of the mantra sounds as distinct balls of light floating across the water over my fingertips into the bowl, over the top of the brass Ganesh.

Playing with water can be so magical, and I am glad I did Ganesh Tarpanam for 45 days. It was a lot of tapas for me and that tapas generated some spiritual experience in the end. I definitely stirred up some prana in my body.

Tarpanam: Water Offering

There is one sort of practice that requires significantly more challenge than the others. In particular, these are the tarpanams. I learned two tarpanams in my ten years of study, and practiced each for forty five days: the first tarpanam was Ganesh Tarpanam; and the second was Sri Bala Tarpanam. Ganesh Tarpanam was for me Phase Four of TJY.

A tarpanam is a water offering to a deity wherein specific Sanskrit mantras are chanted, while offering water from the hands over the deity. Ganapathi Tarpanam or Ganesh Tarpanam was the first tarpanam I learned. It was very interesting and very challenging. Instead of chanting one mantra over and over, there are many lines of mantra that stay the same in some part and change systematically in another part, so that it goes through all the names of all the Shaktis in this way. Then, there is a way it has of running the refrain through the main mantra, word by word. It's like a complicated round. On top of having to get all the chanting right, there is no possibility of being able to memorize it all, at least there was no chance of this for me: I had all the lines of chanting copied onto note cards, and the note cards I wrapped in clear packing tape so they wouldn't get wet and ruined, as I turned through them while my hands were wet from dipping in the water to do the tarpanam.

But. before I learned Ganesh Tarpanam, I had to do Phase Three of Tantric Japa Yoga.

Tantric Japa Yoga, Phase Three

Phase Three of Tantric Japa Yoga is all about Ganesh and Lakshmi.

First, I will talk about Ganesh. But before that I will review what we have talked about so far: First, we talked about Om Namah Shivaya which is Phase One. Then we talked about Om Gayatri Om, which is Phase Two. I also gave out the assignments for Phases One and Two.

In Phase One we meditated on consciousness, pure and simple. Om Namah Shivaya has a plaintive quality to it especially when chanted out loud, and reminds one of how the story of Bhairava is about how we get this longing for God that is like a wolf howling plaintively at the moon. Our wildish souls long for God and in times like this we can chant Om Namah Shivaya to take ourselves to a place beyond this world, beyond our problems, and to bring consciousness into our hearts and our minds to guide us. Shiva is the original guru and it is fitting to start our study with Om Namah Shivaya. We also focus on our third-eye while chanting Om Namah Shivaya, and we focus on the vibration; and do a little bit of pranayama.

In Phase Two we meditated on Om Gayatri Om. We learned that Om is the original vibration and that the Gayatri is the essence of the Vedas; we learned that reading from the Vedas should be preceded and followed by Om and so it is fitting to chant Om before and after the Gayatri Mantra. We meditated on Om as the original vibration, and on how Om vibrates in our body, at the heart, and in the top of the head. And we meditated on this prayer to Gayatri, the feminine light energy of the sun, who is Brahman, intimating that we would like this same consciousness to light our own minds and fill our own hearts and minds and bring us to enlightenment. Gayatri Mantra is truly a prayer for enlightenment which is a prayer to raise the kundalini. We focused on the brow chakra (ajna), while chanting the Gayatri Mantra. Altogether, we focused on three chakras (in an upward progression) during our Om Gayatri Om practice (heart, brow and crown); and Guru Mantra.

Ganesh

Now, we will consider Ganesh. And we will begin with the fact that Ganesh is the Om incarnate. Ganesh is the embodiment of the Om vibration. There is a process of creation that begins with Shiva as pure consciousness and Shakti as pure energy, and when the two come together, the sound is the cosmic vibration, Om. Om starts to vibrate, and in a process that happens over a long time, it divides itself into the 51 letters of the Sanksrit alphabet, and each of those vibrations is also a goddess – a Shakti. Each of those vibrations are responsible for some part of the process of energy and consciousness evolving into matter and being and the entire created world.

Om represents this process of creation which also results in the soul being incarnate in matter, and this is Ganesh: the soul incarnate in matter; the Om incarnate in matter. He is our own soul.

In Hinduism, Ganesh's head represents the soul of man. Indeed, Ganesh is just like us, or we are just like Ganesh. For one thing, Ganesh has the body of a man and the head of an elephant. This symbolizes that as humans we have a big head on our shoulders, which is symbolic of all the capacities of our minds and our ability to expand our awareness and elevate our consciousness. Ganesh is riding on a rat and this symbolizes the nervous system and the reptilian brain or the lower forms of evolution that operate from the more instinctual parts of the brain and do not have the capacities for higher education and expanse of consciousness. That is what human beings are. We have the reptilian brain in us too. Ganesh is riding on a rat, using the rat as a vehicle, which is symbolic again because the Om is incarnate in the nervous system, a sublime subtle spiritual vibration that has its source in Shiva-Shakti, the Ultimate, has taken incarnation into this body which is a nervous system. So, therefore Ganesh has the big head of an elephant, the body of a man, and is riding on a rat, which is relatively small in comparison with the elephant, just as the nervous system is relatively insignificant when considered next to the ultimate consciousness which the mind of man is a doorway to. So, it is a much bigger reality being carried around by our nervous system.

Ganesh has small eyes which means we should concentrate, stay focused and not miss important details. He has big ears which reminds us to be good listeners.

And Ganesh, because he is the incarnation of the Om vibration, which represents the impulse within Shiva-Shakti to evolve into individual beings, represents the impulse to evolve, so it is the urge to move forward. And an elephant is big; he can push forward and push obstacles out of his way.

Ganesh is the remover of obstacles. But Ganesh can place obstacles too. Ganesh is a deity who has roots in a myth about some rambunctious elephants who wreaked a lot of havoc, and evolved into the story we have today of a deity who removes obstacles. However, even to this day, Ganesh can also place obstacles in our path; though we don't hear about this aspect of Ganesh very often, if ever. In Hinduism, Ganesh is mostly invoked in ceremonies that mark the beginning of an endeavor or auspicious event in the hopes of Ganesh's blessings as the remover of obstacles.

You might wonder why Ganesh might place obstacles in our path, but this is because Ganesh may want us to be true to our dharma or our cosmic responsibilities and earthly duties, and Ganesh may want us to be virtuous.

Chanting mantras to Ganesh and doing Ganapathi (another name for Ganesh) Tarpanam, are to please Ganesh so he will rush to our assistance and remove all obstacles for us.

But really, when we pray to Ganesh, on some level, we are asking our own inner self, or our own soul, to oversee our own progress and help us have clear vision and insight, so we can be well prepared and thereby avoid obstacles and pitfalls. Many of the obstacles we wish to remove are within ourselves. Yet our souls have within them the impulse to evolve – to push forward.

Indeed while Ganesh is a very popular deity in Hinduism, he is often not the primary deity of worship. However, there are some in India who worship Ganesh as their primary deity. For them, the emphasis is really on Ganesh as the embodiment of consciousness.

We have to remember that we too are the embodiments of consciousness and energy. Everything in creation is an embodiment of consciousness and energy, from the gross to the subtlest realms, and beyond.

On Ganesh Chaturthi, a popular Hindu holiday celebrating Ganesh, a clay idol of Ganesh is worshiped and then submerged into the river where he dissolves. This is symbolic of the fact that the form is only temporary and when the form dissolves into the river, Ganesh goes back to his formless state.

Energy & Consciousness

We have to remember that the form of the deity is always symbolic in Tantra. The essence of the deity is consciousness and energy or Shiva and Shakti. We refer simply to consciousness knowing that the energy is the energy of consciousness and that consciousness is the consciousness of energy and they are inseparable except that we separate them out to consider them, and in some times, and some places, energy presents itself as more dominant, and in other times and places, consciousness presents as more dominant. Think about the electricity that is running through our walls. We think of it as energy. However it has its own form of consciousness too, because it moves and acts in certain ways with certain properties. That is the limit of its consciousness. Electricity has a limited consciousness that is limited to the structure function and nature of electricity, but we think of it as energy, not as consciousness, although it has consciousness about it.

Now think about the human mind. The human mind manifests as consciousness, which is a sort of mental quality with its own capacities to perform certain functions. We think of it as consciousness, yet because it moves, there has to be energy about it.

This is how Shiva and Shakti operate in Tantric cosmology. They are always intertwined, but sometimes one of them is presenting as more dominant or as the more obvious force. So they are in various things, at various levels, and various mixtures of energy and consciousness. and this is what the Tantric deities are like.

Each of the deities represents some mixture of qualities and moods. Like Bhairava, who is a form of Shiva who represents the feeling of longing that the soul feels for God and is symbolized by a wolf howling at the moon. He is Shiva, but he is a certain mood of consciousness. Same thing with Shaktis, which are specific energies.

We can use prana in the body as an example to illustrate how consciousness and energy are intertwined – how consciousness is energy too, and why sometimes Shakti is called chit – another way of saying energy is consciousness. Prana is the subtle energy of our very own life force and it is very highly conscious. Prana can be compared symbolically to the nervous system of the body, where nerves carry impulses with lightning speed, so that there is no obvious gap between touching something with a finger and feeling the sensation of it in the skin. Our bodies are filled up with energy that can move quickly. Our cells each have energy and consciousness too, that is limited to the function of each specific cell. Electrons know what electrons need to know to be electrons and protons know what protons need to know to be protons. They have energy that can be measured and they are consciousness on some level because they know what their own function is – energy and consciousness woven together for very specific purpose. The energy that keeps everything moving and alive in our bodies is prana. It runs through our nadis as conscious energy, keeping our cells energized, and running through our chakras with purpose. Nadis carry prana as energy that is very conscious that knows what it needs to do and where it needs to go to do it.

We have within us the formless, energized consciousness which has taken form in so many myriad ways.

When we fall asleep at night our minds return to the original source, to the pure field of absolute rest, of absolute Shiva – consciousness. We awaken pranafied – refreshed. Our conscious energy relaxes in deep sleep with no choices to make, and as soon as we wake up, it springs into action having so many decisions to make one after the other throughout our day. It is prana that enables us to move and prana that knows to refresh us and keep us alive in sleep.

Holographic Reality

According to Tantra we are a microcosm of the macrocosm, living in a holographic reality. We are in the image of God, or God is in the image of us, but ultimately we are made out of the same stuff. Our consciousness is limited, but our knowledge of our self can turn within and become aware of deeper levels of consciousness that are closer to the source energy. We can find expanded consciousness. We can be like Ganesh, riding on the rat of our nervous system directing the course with our big well developed minds; and we have the power to turn within and find the formless within us, as energy and consciousness.

As Ganesh moves into the formless in Ganesh Chaturthi, as he dissolves when he is submerged in the water as an idol made of clay or turmeric paste, we move within into the formless aspects of our own nature, and try to connect with the evolutionary energy within us, and carry ourselves forward.

It is also believed that when Ganesh is submerged in the water, obstacles go down with him, are dissolved, and wash away in the river, as Ganesh's symbolic form dissolves in the water.

Ganesh Mantras for the Independent Practitioner

If you are practicing independently and wish to chant a Ganesh Mantra, you can chant:

Om Gam Ganapataye Namaha

However, a different mantra for Ganesh is given with Phase Three of TJY.

If you are interested in taking up the study of TJY, and you want the mantra assignments for Phase Three and beyond, you can reach out directly to the guru. In this chapter, I will share some themes related to the characters in the mantras for Phase Three, who are Ganesh and Lakshmi. And it is my hope that you will feel encouraged to take up the path, or at least will learn something about the rich, complex and ever unfolding story of tantric spirituality.

Lakshmi

Along with Ganesh in Phase Three of Tantric Japa Yoga, we have Lakshmi Mantra. Lakshmi is sometimes depicted seated on the lap of Ganesh. Both Lakshmi and Ganesh are deities of good fortune. Ganesh and Lakshmi are both strongly associated with bodies of water and Lakshmi in particular is associated with rivers in India.

Our next complete to the Goddess, called Devi in India or the Divine Mother, is with Goddess Lakshmi in phase three of Tantric Japa Yoga. Here the basic elements are being laid out for us like cornerstones of a foundation that the rest of the structure will be built upon.

1) First, we have cornerstone of Om Namah Shivaya –
   Consciousness –
   Shiva, the Absolute.

2) Second we have cornerstone of Gayatri Mantra a
   prayer to Divine Kundalini Shakti, the Divine Mother
   as Brahman, and Light.

3) Third, we have corner stone of Ganesh or Ganapathi,
   who is Om incarnate. Om the Pranava, the formless
   Divine, embodied in the form of an elephant headed
   man, the remover of obstacles, and the evolutionary
   force within our very souls.

4) Fourth, we have Cornerstone of Goddess, and in this
   case we are considering Goddess Lakshmi – who is
   very important because of how she cares about our
   worldly success. All Goddesses by all names are
   Shakti, and the Divine Mother is none other than
   Brahman herself.

   Goddess Lakshmi is often depicted with gold
coins, and is often seated in the center of a lotus
blossom, with lotus flowers in one of her hands. The
lotus flower is symbolic of spirituality. The root is in
the mud, below the water; the vine crawls up to the
top of the water; and the flower blooms on top of the
water. This is symbolic of the spiritual awakening
process in humans. The lotus flower is also very
ephemeral, blossoming only in the daytime, then
closing up on itself and sinking back below the
surface of the water, down into the mud overnight,
and coming back up to the surface in the daylight to
bloom again.

Goddess Lakshmi has the form of a woman and all women and girls are considered embodiments of Goddess Lakshmi. This Goddess is also a champion of women and girls. The Lakshmi Tantra clearly states that the yogi who desires the favor of Goddess Lakshmi should not abuse women in any way and should treat women like divinity, with respect.

Goddess Lakshmi is different from Goddess Kali who destroys all our attachments. Goddess Lakshmi wants us to enjoy the earthly existence. She wants us to have abundance and even wealth. She surely wants us to have all we need to live life comfortably. She represents wealth, abundance, prosperity, and good fortune. Good fortune includes a wide range of areas that Lakshmi can help us with.

Lakshmi is associated with nature and especially with rivers and streams and with the beloved Tulsi plant.

Lakshmi likes cleanliness and orderliness.

Diwali, a holiday that features Lakshmi, also features lighting lots of candles to dispel darkness and light the way of Goddess Lakshmi. People clean house, paint their walls, sweep off the front porch and put rangoli or chalk paintings of lotus flowers and mandalas to invite the devi.

In spite of the fact that Goddess Lakshmi is the goddess of wealth, prosperity and abundance, she does not give out wealth indiscriminately. She helps us in our path. If we chant Lakshmi Mantra, we are asking Laskmi to help us to succeed, in life, in whatever endeavor we are petitioning her about. She can help us with all sorts of things and there are various versions of Lakshmi to address certain specific concerns. But, what is most important is to realize that Goddess Lakshmi can be sought for support for a wide variety of problems and issues related to our desire to thrive in the material world – in physical creation. Lakshmi doesn't want us to suffer. She wants us to be the best we can be.

When we petition Goddess Lakshmi through mantra, we are aligning our vibration with her vibration through the mantra, and so we can meditate on all the qualities that Lakshmi likes. She likes us to take care of ourselves and beautify ourselves, to dress ourselves so that our appearance reflects joy, beauty, and abundance, adorning ourselves with clean clothes, if not new clothes, then at least not torn. She likes us to sweep off our front stoop, and paint a little rangoli on the front stoop, to welcome divinity into the home, and also as good energy to greet guests to the home. Lakshmi also likes it when we take good care of our guests and treat them like royalty.

If we think of all the things that Lakshmi likes, she likes us to be good in keeping account of our own business. Whether it is an actual business, or the business of cooking or cleaning or doing the laundry or shopping or doing any creative project or job, Lakshmi is all about wanting us to do our best, to be on top of our game, and to attend to the details, so that everything is clean, orderly, and beautiful.

If we start to chant to Goddess Lakshmi and we want her to help us in business, we will naturally start thinking of things we can do to help ourselves succeed better. This is in line with aligning our vibration to the vibration of the goddess. If we like what she likes and attend to what she concerns herself with, we will be doing good management of our affairs and keeping our business in order. Taking good care of our clients. Taking care of all the details. Being sure to present ourselves well and to have beautiful wares or services to provide, not shabby or sub-quality – Lakshmi wouldn't like that. She loves beauty and abundance and treating guests with honor and respect, and so in a business we should treat our clients likewise.

Lakshmi can also help us quicken our intellect, which we need in order to succeed in life. She helps us stay on top of our game.

And we should also remember that Goddess Lakshmi is also Shakti or the Divine Mother: or Divine Energy, Consciousness and Being.

The point is, as Shakti, Lakshmi is the Divine Mother. She's not just a talisman for luck.

Dharma, Artha, Kama, Moksha: Four Arms of Lakshmi

In Hinduism and in Tantra there are considered to be four goals in human life. Goddess Lakshmi has four hands and each of her hands symbolizes one of these four goals:

1) **Dharma** (righteousness, moral values)
2) **Artha** (prosperity, economic values)
3) **Kama** (the pursuit of pleasure, love and psychological values)
4) **Moksha** (the pursuit of spiritual liberation)

Goddess Lakshmi does not just want us to be rich. She knows that we have to succeed in this life as well, and the prosperity and economic aspect is also important; so she wants to help us with it. She knows that we need to be in alignment with dharma so that we can attract good karma as we go through life, and avoid creating bad karma for ourselves, so she wants to help us be righteous, not just to have money. According to Devdutt Pattanaik in his book on Lakshmi, this goddess does not want a few to hoard wealth, and she cares about the fair distribution of wealth.

She also wants us to be successful in growing spiritually and evolving ourselves to be the best that we can be. This is why we petition her also with mantra, which is an act of righteousness.

Goddess Lakshmi knows that in this school of life we also want to succeed in kama or the pursuit of pleasure, love, and good psychology. She doesn't want us to be suffering abuse of any form. She doesn't want to see us being oppressed. She wants us to have good relations, love and healthy psychology.

And last but not least, Goddess Lakshmi knows that we are all on the path to moksha. It takes us lifetimes to evolve in the school of life. However, while we are evolving our spiritual selves, she wants us to succeed in this life as it is the springboard of learning and from here we raise ourselves up to the challenge of seeking spiritual liberation. In fact climbing on the ladder of life to a modicum of success can create the conditions for spiritual pursuit.

When we are bogged down, constantly in fear of not having enough food, a place to live, or safety, we have a hard time finding the personal space to do spiritual practices to lift ourselves up. We get dragged down by the dramas of life and need some sort of safe container within which we can regularly and consistently go within to meditate and to experience our inner world. Lakshmi wants us to have prosperity in terms of spiritual pursuits as well. Prosperity, having enough, having a safe place to be, having emotional supports and not being in situations where others are constantly dragging us down, are all important, so Lakshmi cares about all of this.

Lakshmi cares about us achieving moksha. And what is moksha? Moksha is liberation, but what is it liberation from?

Moksha is for one thing, liberation from the cycle of rebirth. And how do we achieve this liberation? We achieve liberation according to Tantra, by becoming aware of consciousness as the source, of consciousness as God, of consciousness as the essential element of our own makeup. In other words, we become aware that "Who We Are," is a microcosm of the macrocosm, of the ultimate consciousness and source of all creation. We are made of the same stuff. No we are not God, in the sense that we cannot hold the whole world in existence as God does – or even our own physical body. God, or Shiva, is consciousness that is very specifically aware of everything in a distinct way, and is holding all of creation in its conscious grasp, and holding it all in existence. We can't do that. We are made of the same consciousness but it is limited to expressing itself through the vehicles of our bodies and minds. So even when a person realizes oneness with absolute consciousness, they still get up in the morning and have breakfast and fill their days with the things that need to be done, and live out their earthly life. Absolute consciousness is not just aware in a vague way. It's as aware of me sitting here as it is aware of you sitting there. It has this great of a magnificent scope. God is a vast all-encompassing, never ending consciousness, energy and being that is beyond our ability to comprehend. We can unite Shiva and Shakti in the crown and experience that consciousness while we are yet living, and this is called moksha or the liberation from the cycle of rebirth. We are made of the same stuff as the Ultimate, and we experience through our limited context, but through meditation and activating prana and kundalini within we can come eventually to a state where we can have an experience of expanded consciousness and experience our oneness with the Divine.

Lakshmi cares about this. What proof can I give that Lakshmi cares? She cares that we evolve because the evolutionary force is within us for a reason. We are endowed with the capacity to liberate ourselves from the confines of discursive thinking and access an expanded consciousness and Lakshmi wants us to succeed in this too.

We can seek out Goddess Lakshmi for full support. We can ask her support in all matters of life: dharma, artha, kama, and moksha. Chanting her mantra, we can vibrate on her wavelength and become one with Goddess Lakshmi.

Lakshmi Mantras for Independent Practice

If you are practicing independently, you can use either of these two mantras for Lakshmi:

Om Sri Maha Lakshmyai Namaha

Or

Om Shreem Hreem Shreem

Kamale Kamalalaye, Praseeda praseeda,

Om Shredm Hreem Shreem

Shri Maha Lakshmi Devyai Namaha

In TJY the mantras given are different mantras than what is found on the internet.

If you want to continue on with TJY, you can get those mantra assignments from the guru.

Chapter Eleven:

Phase Five and Beyond:

Divine Mother – Goddess

Growing up I was raised Christian, Lutheran to be precise. At some point, as far back as I can remember, we were attending the Lutheran church, and in my most recent memory it was an ELCA Lutheran church. ELCA is the most liberal branch of Lutherans. ELCA started incorporating inclusive language years ago, in step with society, while other denominations rejected options for change in the direction of being more inclusive: ELCA allowed women in higher roles in the church administration, as well as allowing women to be ministers; and ELCA Lutherans were among the first Christian denominations to ordain openly gay clergy. When I went to college, there was an ELCA Lutheran center on campus, called Luther House, and I attended their Wednesday evening services and even went on a field trip up north, with two other students, to the Lutheran Student Movement Convention in Bozeman, Montana.

I felt detached and uninvolved at the Lutheran Student Movement National Convention, and remember the first night there, awake while my roommate slept, I stood in the dark, with insomnia, at the window in our room, gazing out across the campus fields of grass in the dark. Then, on the last day of the convention, we were all in a church sanctuary, sitting side by side in the pews, and in spite of the fact that I loved Jesus, as the ministers were talking, I was distracted and started to slouch down in my seat on the wooden pew. Then the next speaker took the podium, and it was a minister with a beard, from Alaska, who started, in the middle of his talk, referring to God as She, and suddenly I found myself sitting upright in my seat. That glorious moment was short lived and we all filed out of the sanctuary to our respective rides for the trip home, and my life went on as usual, mostly without any Divine Feminine themes.

Let us now explore the topic of the Divine Mother, of Devi, of Sri Mata, of Shakti. There are so many names of the Divine Mother that I don't know where to begin. She is a big topic. And she is very important.

The Divine Feminine is important to me because I am a woman and we all want to see ourselves reflected back to us. It makes me feel included in the divine scheme of things to imagine a feminine aspect or face of divinity. Even men can enjoy relating to God through the archetype of the Mother. In reality we have different genders, so it is a balanced reflection of reality when Divinity is depicted as having both masculine and feminine faces.

There was another woman, a college student, who attended at Luther House, who also liked the divine feminine, and she would mention it from time to time, that God could be a woman – a divine feminine force. And the minister would oblige her and instead of saying Our Father who art in heaven, in our little group of a handful of worshipers, we prayed "Abba/Imma in heaven," which means, Father and Mother in Heaven. In fact the minister at the time explained to us how Abba really meant papa, and

Imma was mama, and what familiar terms these were, and how nice it was to take such a familiar tone with God, and to include God in his/her entirety as containing both masculine and feminine divine energies.

This is a concept that is common in Tantra. There is a form of Shiva called Shiva Ardhinara in which half the image is Lord Shiva in his male bodied aspect, and the other half of the same body/image is Shatki in her female bodied aspect. Indeed, in Tantra, God is beyond our fathoming, is all encompassing, and is expressed in story as masculine and feminine archetypes. In fact, these masculine and feminine counterparts of Tantra do not fit neatly into what we might think of as gender stereotypes.

The question arises of what it means to be archetypally feminine or archetypally masculine.

In Tantra it simple means that the Deity is seen as being embodied in the body of a man or the body of a woman. Deities which are embodied in the body of a woman are called goddesses, or devis. Deities which are depicted as embodied in the body of a man are called gods, or devs. The absolute Brahman is beyond qualities or limitations and has no gender, is pure absolute consciousness. And out of Brahman we have Shiva and Shakti of Tantra, where Shiva is consciousness and Shakti is energy.

There are many names and forms of Shiva and there are many names and forms of Shakti. These names and forms represent various moods or aspects of the deity, or special functions.

We have seen some of the other divine forms, like Lord Shiva, and Ganesh, and we have seen some divine feminine Forms, such as Gayatri and Goddess Lakshmi.

In fact, a lot of focus has been put on the divine feminine in India and there are many important aspects of the Goddess, who is lovingly referred to as Divine Mother. Divine Mother gives creative energy to consciousness and thereby causes all of the creation to happen. In fact, she is very powerful and in some aspects is depicted as slaying demons; so she is not "feminine" in a stereotypical sense, at least not exclusively.

The counterpart to Lord Shiva is Goddess Shakti, who takes on many forms. As Shakti she is energy and as some of her derivative embodiments, she assumes certain moods or archetypes.

For female divine feminine archetypes we have so far encountered Goddess Lakshmi and Goddess Gayatri. Now we are about encounter the Matrika, and to meet the cast of Sri Vidya. But before all that, let's talk a little bit about Goddess Durga, because she is the very tough Goddess who destroys the demons. Durga is a warrior and a fierce protector, whereas Lakshmi is graceful and benevolent. One of our phases in Tantric Japa Yoga deals with the Sri Navakshari Mantra and that is our introduction to Goddess Durga.

Then right before we go into the Sri Vidya, study of Sri Mata, we meet Sri Bala the nine-year-old Goddess who is daughter of Sri Maha Tripurasundari, and who is like our young, spiritual self who is just setting out on the path, or like our magical inner-child. This nine-year-old is very self-contained and wise for her age and she already has mastery of certain powers and influences. She is the Divine Child in female form. I enjoyed connecting with Sri Bala.

The TJY practice for Sri Bala was a beautiful Tarpanam. For Sri Bala Tarpanam, I had to draw a yantra on the water. I was gaining more endurance in sitting to do the work of tarpanam, and I was particularly intrigued by the fact that there is this child Goddess, because I was raised Christian and I am very familiar with the child God Jesus. This Child Goddess, Sri Bala, is the introduction to the Sri Vidya series. Sri Vidya is the study of Sri Mata, the Great Mother, and is something I practiced as part of Tantric Japa Yoga assignments from Shajesh.

But first, we have Matrika Nyasa, which for me was Phase Five of Tantric Japa Yoga.

Matrika Nyasa: TJY Phase Five

We have learned that Ganesh is the embodiment of the Om vibration. We have learned that the Om vibration evolves into the 51 letters of the Sanskrit alphabet, which is a process that takes thousands of years. And this is where we find ourselves now, as we begin to consider the topic of the Divine Mother: we find ourselves here on the verge of Matrika Nyasa, wherein the letters of the Sanskrit alphabet form the sound body of the Divine Mother. According to Tantra, as the Om, the original cosmic word explodes out into 51 letters of the Sanskrit alphabet, this first explosion of Creation – the big bang – is the chief goddess of Sri Vidya, known as Sri Maha Tripurasundari.

I have to pause here to consider how much this really is. We have here such a rich exposition of Hindu Tantric Cosmological detail. It's awesome. As I look over the Fifth Phase of Tantric Japa Yoga, "Matrika Nyasa (Divinising the Body)" – it's beautiful. No wonder I felt so astounded to be given such beautiful assignments imparting a rich knowledge of tradition and a lot of details to explore. To be honest with you, I am still learning. What I am giving here is a humble overview of this topic based on my experience and research.

The story goes that the Om was the original vibration and from the Om, which was already Shiva and Shakti together, 51 more shaktis emanated and together comprise the sound body of the Goddess. This is because it is the Goddess herself, broken down into individual precise packets of energy and consciousness. Even when we are considering something as energy, still consciousness is there if that energy is specialized to do anything at all. It is consciousness that creates specialized knowledge in the energy packet to accomplish what it wants to accomplish. Basically, as energy from the Goddess emanates into each of the letters of the Sanskrit alphabet, each letter is another Goddess. You could say in a way that the pure sound when followed back to its source into the Goddess is light, and she is light like a million suns, so bright, and each of the letters of the Sanskrit alphabet is a ray of light – a specialized Shakti with a specialized function – little goddess energies. And I say little euphemistically, because these are all great powers and some of the original phenomenon from which the whole creation evolved. Each of the Sanskrit letters does its own job and through their combined work, eventually physical matter is created, and consciousness embodies as individual souls in matter.

Let's pause here and consider these matrikas and consider Matrika Nyasa and what it is, since Matrika Nyasa is phase five of Tantric Japa Yoga. Now we have come a long way and we are going to do a nyasa. In fact, Matrika Nyasa is not the only nyasa to be done in Tantric Japa Yoga. However Matrika Nyasa is the first, and the other nyasas don't come until later in the program: all are beautiful.

Nyasas

Nyasas are very important in Tantra and involve the placement, through the use of a mudra (hand gesture), of mantras, on specific places of the body. When we say that a mantra is placed at the specific places of the body, in this case we are using the names of God, or in the case of Matrika Nyasa, of Goddess; Sanskrit letters are individual vibrations of the individual Shaktis. So, there is the preamble that goes out before the name, and then the name, or in this case the vibration, and ending with namah. So one goes through all the letters of the Sanskrit alphabet one by one, placing each one in its appropriate place on the body. This process is a process of placing light in and on the body, as Shakti energies are rays of Shakti light, which is what the pure form of the vibration dissolves into: pure light. It is a specific vibration yes, which can be thought of or visualized as a ray of light. It is a conscious packet of energy, or Shakti.

So with the Matrika Nyasa practice we divinise our body, by infusing it with these divine energies – which are rays of divine light.

There are two forms of the nyasa, namely inner and outer. The outer nyasa places the energies on points on the surface of the body, and the inner nyasa places the energies within the body on points in the chakras.

Each chakra is visualized as a flower having a specific number of petals, and each of the petals of each of the flowers has one of the Sanskrit letters on it, considering all the six chakras below sahasrara but not including sahasrara. So chakras one through six have all the letters of the Sanskrit alphabet divided onto their 50 petals. And the sahasrara or the crown chakra has all 51 letters going around the top of the head, which is symbolic of the fact that the sahasrara is infinity. There are 1,000 petals but we don't count to 1,000; we count to 51 which consists of the entirety of the Divine Mother in all her glory, and also symbolizes infinity. The base chakra, muladhara has four petals. Next is Swadhisthana with six petals. Manipura has ten petals. Anahata has twelve. Vishuddhi has sixteen petals, and ajna chakra has two petals.

Sri Vidya

After Matrika Nyasa, and a few other phases, comes Sri Bala Tarpanam. Then, after Sri Bala Tarpanam comes the entire Shri Vidya, which is the study of Sri Mata, the Divine Mother, or put simply Sri Vidya is the study of the Divine Mother, Sri Maha Tripurasundari, the goddess of the three worlds. However in the Shri Vidya she is referred to also as Shodashi, which is another name for Sri Maha Tripurasundari, who is also known as the shining one.

Sri Maha Tripurasundari is the Divine Mother in all Her glory. At the beginning of the universe when the first vibration happened and there was a big explosion of a big Om vibration, that first explosion of energy and consciousness was the Goddess Sri Maha Tripurasundari, and the entire creation comes from her creative activity

Sri Maha Tripurasundari is also more than just this explosion of Creation. Just like Shiva, She is cit or energy and consciousness that is beyond our conception, which created the whole world. In her saguna form, Sri Maha Tripurasundari is a beautiful woman and the mother of Sri Bala. In her Nirguna or formless aspect she is beyond our conception and is responsible for the creation, and is Mother of the three worlds.

Sri Maha Tripurasundari is conscious energy. She is energy being and bliss. Pure consciousness is bliss. Pure consciousness is light. Pure consciousness and pure energy, evolving over thousands of years, evolving, from the first explosion of creation, is a conscious Goddess who has knowledge of me sitting here right now, whose invisible eyes and ears are throughout invisible space. Who knows that I am sitting here typing. Who cares. Who wants us to evolve and find our way back to the source, to God consciousness, which is pure radiant light and pure being. We know Divine Mother wants us to find our way back to the source, because she has created us such that this is an innate potential within us.

We are made out of the same consciousness and energy as Shiva and Shakti, and we can experience expanded awareness. We are energy and consciousness and being and bliss and we have to rediscover all this.

Sri Maha Tripurasundari, beautiful Goddess of the three worlds, embodies all of creation, and is the primary goddess of Sri Vidya – known as Shodashi in Sri Vidya and also as Tripurasundari. All the other goddesses in Sri Vidya are seen as being part of the total energy of the Great Goddess Shodashi or Sri Maha Tripurasundari. Each of these ten Goddesses embodies a certain mood or certain qualities – its own archetype of the divine feminine. There are a number of works that go into some detail on the ten mahavidyas. I am not going to go into great detail here but will touch on each one briefly. Also, Shajesh offers an online course on the Ten Mahavidyas, or the Ten Goddesses of Sri Vidya. The course is listed on his website which is given in the preface to this book. The course title is: Dasha Maha Vidyas.

These are the ten Goddesses of Sri Vidya:

1. **Kali** – Kali is a slayer of demons. When Durga could not kill the demons because they had become too powerful, Kali burst out of the center of Durga's brow. Kali was strong enough to kill all the demons. As the demons died, each drop of their blood would spring to life as a new demon, as the drop of blood touched the ground. Kali stuck out her long tongue and caught every last drop of blood before it hit the ground. Kali destroys darkness. She is a fierce mother who protects those who love her. Kali is also "she who is greater than time."

2. **Tara** – is a very mysterious goddess who stands at the edge of a lake at night. It's dark and there is some moonlight. You want to cross the lake and she is there in a boat, and she takes you across. She helps us navigate the way in the dark. She is also said to help souls cross over the lake of death.

3. **Bhuvaneshwari**—Bhuvaneshwari represents space, and also the space of our hearts and our own spiritual growth. She removes obstacles and gives courage and confidence. She is seen as an incarnation of Adi Shakti – the supreme, primordial Mother.

4. **Bhairavi** – Bhairavi is the consort of Bhairava, the very terrifying aspect of Lord Shiva, and as such she herself is a very terrifying form of the Goddess, much like Goddess Kali. She wants us to be free from fear. She terrifies demons and chases them away.

5. **Chinnemasta** – Chinnemasta is the Goddess who cuts off her own head. This symbolizes cutting off the discursive mind and connecting to the power within, or to kundalini awakening.

6. **Dhumavati** – Dhumavati is old and ugly and often is depicted in the cremation ground. She is all that is unwanted and cast away in society, and all that is inauspicious. She points us in the direction of the Divine when there is no solace or comfort in living.

7. **Bagalamukhi** – Bagalamukhi is depicted with the tongue of the demon in her hand, and has the power to silence and immobilize our enemies.

8. **Matangi** –Matangi arises out of the table scraps of Shiva and Parvati (a form of Shakti who is Shiva's spouse). The first thing Matangi, a fair woman, asks for is the scraps of leftover food, at the table where some of the gods are dining. Matangi breaks taboo by taking leftover food. She breaks the taboos of the purity cult.

9. **Kamala** – Kamala means lotus and she is the lotus Goddess. Kamala is really another name for Goddess Lakshmi in her tantric form as one of the Sri Vidya Goddesses. Kamala hints at more independence, whereas Lakshmi is married to Vishnu or Naryana.

10. **Shodashi** – Shodashi is Tripurasundari the Queen of Heaven, and the main top Goddess of Shri Vidya. She is ruler of the three worlds.

Part Three:
Spiritual Experiences and Conclusion

Introduction to Part Three

Part Three is where we wrap it all up.

Chapter Twelve consists of reflections on spiritual experiences I have had in the context of various practices. Spiritual experiences may be part of life and are invited in Tantric Japa Yoga practice. I take a multi-disciplinary approach here, because I explore experiences I've had doing other spiritual practices throughout my life, as well as those I've had in the context of doing Tantric Japa Yoga. This can highlight for us how various practices can support us in different ways, and is a reminder that in life, we don't have to be purists about our spiritual search: we can use any and all tools at our disposal in the service of our personal and spiritual growth, including practices independent of or in addition to TJY. When I first took up instruction with Shajesh, one of the things he said to me was that there are many paths, and people are drawn to different sorts of practices depending on their own tendencies and nature – according to their own vibration – and it's ok. TJY is one path, with an elaborate system of practices, intended to evolve the practitioner spiritually. I have continued to do other practices while actively pursuing Tantric Japa Yoga, and find that combining practices gives me a rich web of self-support.

Finally, in the Conclusion, I make closing remarks about my spiritual search and the role that TJY has played in my own life.

Chapter Twelve:
Spiritual Experience

Early on in my Tantric Japa Yoga studies, Shajesh recommended I keep a journal and record my experiences. Indeed Hinduism and Tantra both appreciate the value of dreams and spiritual experiences, which are part of the mind and may contain insights and divine revelation, as well as content of the processing mind, and insights into the psyche for self-study.

In Hinduism and in Tantra there are four states of consciousness, which are: waking; dreaming; deep (dreamless) sleep; and the fourth state, called turiya, which is like pure awareness. In the context of Hinduism and Tantra, dreamlike and spiritual experiences are seen as part of the path to spiritual transformation and help us see through the veil of Maya. In fact, self-realization means to realize the self, and that is the whole self. The dreaming mind, spiritual experiences, and meaningful coincidences (synchronicity) may be seen as manifestations of the divine. When we are in deep, dreamless sleep, it is believed we are one with ultimate consciousness.

If, by design experiences come to us, they are part of the process and we can enjoy them. Lord Shiva is also Lord of the Dance. He is Shiva Nataraja, dancing out all the yoga poses, and we can follow him as he dances his way into meditation. We can take our time and enjoy smelling the flowers along the way. We don't have to shirk our own spiritual experience, as if that is what is holding us back.

I've been doing practices of one sort or another, and having spiritual experiences, since early college, and it is meaningful to me to consider all my spiritual experience so that my 10+ years of Tantric Japa Yoga practice and experience is seen in the broader context of my whole life. And, to highlight that the spiritual experiences I did have, did happen in the context of various practices. This is a topic that feeds into knowing ourselves. On the one hand we don't have to make too much of our spiritual experiences, since we know the ultimate goal is spiritual growth and enlightenment. On the other hand, this is part of who we are and acknowledging the more intuitive dimensions of our experience can give us a sense of the mystical, the metaphysical, and the hidden layers of the mind. And sometimes other practices may help us as well. So many things can contribute to our unfolding.

This chapter is my experience journal, including experiences all the way back to the early college, years before TJY, as well as my TJY experience.

Early Years

When I was in college, I had a few spiritual experiences, and I do not know if kundalini was involved. I definitely had a few trance experiences in the simple resting meditation I was doing; and one time I went into a state and could feel the energy rushing through my body in circuits. When energy is rushing through the nadis, that is prana rushing through the nadis, and there is a vast network of nadis rushing pranic energy through the body at all times. So maybe that is what I experienced. I had a couple of other experiences as well. One time I was resting on my back and I fell into an energy trance: my eyes were closed and I couldn't move, yet I felt aware of my body and awake mentally – a state that was somewhere between waking and sleep, wherein my awareness felt itself to be inside my head, which felt like a space as vast as the universe. When I came out of it and opened my eyes, my arms were dangling above me as if I did not need to hold them up, and I thought to myself "oh, I forgot to take my arms down." For three days after this when I looked into people's eyes, I saw the same field of electrically charged energy that I had seen in my mind's eye in that trance state. What was that? The world may never know. Was it prana moving through my system creating that experience? I never had another experience like it, and I never experienced anything I would call kundalini energy until about two years ago.

Resting with Being and Eye Movements

During the time when I was on the internet in groups, I came to know a woman who taught me a technique for emotional processing. She said I should rest in a comfortable position, close the eyes and relax the breath; while breathing, move eyes back and forth, behind the closed lids, rapidly or slowly; and while the eyes move, let thoughts and feelings flow. She likened this to a sort of REM processing. I have used this technique often, modifying it to suit me.

I like to rest on my side with a pillow under the side of my head, knees bent a little, top arm resting on a pillow, with that one hand close to my face, sometimes touching my heart chakra as I breathe. Resting in this position, I tune into the breath right away and be sure to let the breath flow freely. I notice what the breath feels like, and feelings express through the quality of the breath. Eyes may be moving back and forth, slowly, and sometimes I forget about the eyes and it becomes more about the breath. Although if the breath becomes stuck, remembering to move the eyes, can help. I follow the breath to see what it reveals to me – hidden tension, sadness or other feelings that I have been unconsciously suppressing or unaware of. I observe the quality of my experience, feeling with psyche, heart and mind. These sessions are great for emotional processing and releasing tension.

The other night I was resting in this way, releasing the breath. So much goes out on the exhale. Letting go. Letting all the images flow through me with empathy, listening and observing. I was feeling with my adult self, at first, but my experience started to morph and change as I breathed, flowing with feeling. Then, I felt such a poignant and lucid immediacy with my younger self, who was feeling very vulnerable. And as I breathed with my inner-child, feeling, I had a sudden dreamlike experience of myself as a ray of light, embodied as a little girl – and I realized that as a little child, I was already the essence of Lord Shiva. This experience produced beautiful energy in my system, of love, light, and peace. I felt tingly all over and had an immense sense of compassion with my own soul. Healing is a process. In that moment something in me took part in healing and moved forward.

If you have been processing a lot and need to rest the mind, place the palm of your hand on your forehead, with the heel of your hand at the eyebrows. Rest and breathe.

Shamanism

It was in the early part of this century, in 2002, when I had been exploring shamanism through reading and online in Yahoo groups. A woman I met in groups, who I respected, referred me to a real shaman who she said was in the top two percent of gifted shamans. This woman was working as both an astrologer and as a shaman doing soul retrievals. She was working with a group of shamans who did soul retrieval work for a Metis Native Woman, a shaman, who had given some of them their training. However the woman I consulted, Grace, was also a Hawaiian Kahuna who had studied in Hawaii with a respected teacher. For those who are not familiar with soul retrieval, it is a spiritual art wherein the shaman journeys for the client, identifies aspects of the self that have split off as a result of trauma, and brings them back to the client, blowing them into the body, for integration. There is a 30 day integration process. I had four soul retrievals over a period of about a year and a half, and after the fourth one, Grace told me that I now had enough experience so that I could recognize my own soul parts and welcome them back to myself if I do. Now, as I write this book, I am experiencing a spontaneous soul retrieval since a few days ago. This soul retrieval is a gift and is a sudden shift in my energy and awareness. I am taking myself through the integration process with it. It is amazing and I credit this new healing to kundalini being active in me and moving me in the path of spiritual growth. Fred Alan Wolf, theoretical quantum physicist and consciousness researcher, says in his book, *The Spiritual Universe,* that soul loss is the same as being cut off from certain parts of our awareness – certain parts of our imaginal realm – and that soul retrieval amounts to regaining access to such lost areas of experience.

Certainly this qualifies as more in the department of svadhyaya or self-study.

Solar Healing

I tried sungazing for some years and really enjoyed that. I stumbled onto a sungazing forum on the internet and actually ended up talking to HRM (Sunyogi Hira Ratan Manek) and Sunyogi Umasankar, through email of course. I did sungazing for years, until one day, having stood to gaze for 50 minutes from 10 am, in the New Mexico morning sun, I felt something like a jolt of lightning, or electricity, jolt from the back of my eyes, across the top of my head branching out. I was sore to the touch a little on the top of my head for a few days and when I tried to gaze again I experienced a lesser degree of the same thing, so after all the years of sungazing I stopped. I still look at the sun sometimes, but don't do regular gazing. The sun is a powerful symbol in Tantra. In the Gayatri Mantra it is a symbol of and a bringer of awakening. Solar energy wakes up our whole planet, and wakes up prana in the body, which stimulates spiritual growth.

Synchronicity

One time, in my thirties, when my life was very busy, I was resting in meditation and I had this sudden vision experience, wherein I felt like my head was inside the head of an eagle. It was a vision of overlapping auras, as if the spirit double or ghostly twin of an eagle was occupying the same space as my head. Then in my mind a voice said "I will be there." I got up from my meditation and went out on my daily bike ride. Out on the desert, out past the end of town, and as I was going down a long hill, suddenly a large shadow fell on me. I stopped to look up and see what it was. A big desert eagle was perched on the top of a power pole there, and as I stood staring at it, it turned its head to the side so I was able to see its profile, then it alighted off the pole and flew in a big circle around the sky overhead. I got on my bike and rode off.

I encountered another eagle shortly after that. I was riding my bike on the desert and my dog Sasha was with me, a Dalmation. We were riding along on a sand road and I stopped, because there was something large by the side of the road just ahead of us. It was a big bird – another desert eagle – this one, eating a prey. Sasha stopped too and stood beside me, looking in the direction of the big bird. It was so big. We watched together for brief, yet timeless moments. Then the bird slowly lifted up, took to flight, and we continued on our way.

Two experiences. I did not analyze them for meaning but it seemed to me that I had some sort of psychic experience involving a mental connection with eagles and I never saw a wild eagle before that in all my life and never have seen one again. It certainly was synchronicity, and it points to the idea that on the subtler levels we are all connected in some way.

We are part of a web of life. We can understand some of this with science, such as how we breathe in what plants breathe out, while plants breathe in what we breathe out, and how we need sunshine, water and food for life. Tantra also considers synchronicity to be meaningful and sees it as a manifestation of the interconnectedness of life on all levels, even the subtle intuitive levels. We are part of not just a larger ecosystem but of a larger consciousness – a big mind – according to Hinduism and Tantra. Fred Alan Wolf, theoretical quantum physicist and consciousness researcher, gets close to some of this in his book *The Dreaming Universe: a mind expanding journey into the realms where psyche and physics meet*. These quantum realms and realities belong to Lord Shiva, Tripurasundari, the Divine Mother, and even to Ganesh.

Relaxation, Refreshment, Energy

Then, I took a course wherein I learned a pranayama breathing practice of a popular Indian guru that I did daily for years. I participated in satsangs with a group of others and we all would do the long kriya to the tape with the guru's voice on it, guiding us through the practice. I never had any kundalini experiences that I am aware of while doing the pranayama, or any dramatic spiritual experience, but it was calming and it helped me get through my life and start to heal from so much, and I'm positive it was good for my lungs. The physical benefits of meditation and pranayama are real.

TJY Experiences

If you want a reliable way to work on your energy body through spiritual practices, Tantric Japa Yoga is a very good system that progresses the student along a trajectory. I felt noticeable shifts in my mental energy and my ability to cope with various things in my life, right from the outset, and as I moved through my Tantric Japa training, I sure felt the vibration. When I was doing the bed-time meditation after a while I started to feel as if I could see through my closed eyelids in the dark. I tested this and it sure seemed as if I could see my hand moving in front of my face with my eyes closed and no lights on in the room. Maybe not miraculous, but a refined sense of visual focus?

When I was doing Ganesh Tarpanam, I felt energy like bells skipping over my fingertips into the bowl of water as I chanted, but I'm not sure if I would say that was kundalini and it didn't occur to me at the time. It was clear I was energized from the chanting, and probably had activated a lot of prana in my system, and I felt a certain activation in the base so maybe it was kundalini starting to be activated. However, it never occurred to me it might be kundalini. I'm not sure why it didn't occur to me. It was just the one isolated experience and it was so faint, not like what I have been experiencing in the past two years, I will assume it was Pranashakti constellating in my base chakra and maybe she was trying to wake up kundalini.

I didn't really feel what I started to consciously identify as being kundalini until about my eigth year of practice, when I had taken an almost yearlong break from chanting for a while – the only really long break I had taken from chanting in all the time I'd been studying with Shajesh. I started back up with my chanting, and right away I started to experience energy in my body and for some reason at that point, I realized it was kundalini in my body – and in part because the energy was stronger, more noticeable – like an energy I had never felt before in my body, that kept returning with each day of practice. I have decided I will call these new sensations the "subtle energy of the vibration," or the "subtle vibration of the mantra."

Subtle Energy and Kundalini

Even when I started to feel the subtle vibration of the mantra while chanting my daily practice, it did not right away occur to me that I was experiencing kundalini. It began to dawn on me though as the experience continued over the next year, getting stronger at times and more pervasive throughout my practice. Then, at some point, I occasionally started to experience the subtle vibrations of the mantra at other times (i.e. while not chanting). I began to notice that if I chanted mantra as I was going about my day, that the subtle vibration of the mantra would come back. And one day when energy was high, I had a very good session of chanting, and at the end, when I started to do my breathing exercise, I felt a sudden whoosh of energy and bright white light rush up into my head into the frontal region. This was my experience of it. I have been feeling more head experiences and sensations while chanting and immediately after chanting, so I know I am on the path and kundalini is doing its work in me. However, I expect my experience may fluctuate and change over time.

I have often felt even from the beginning, that after chanting there is a subtle dizziness in the head, but it was so mild, and I suspect it was prana, or just a vibrating sensation in my head from all the real vibrations in the physical realm from chanting out loud. I just read an article the other day about a new discovery in science that is groundbreaking that shows that our brains use small electrical fields that are close enough to be in contact with one another to pass information through these electrical networks in the brain, activity which it was formerly believed was done by the neurons and synapses. Scientists couldn't figure out with neurons having to cross synapses to receptors, how the brain could think as fast as it does. With this new discovery, they have made new calculations and it totally accounts for how fast the brain works. So if we have electrical networks in our brain that are so subtle and small and the chanting is creating vibrations, who knows how this is affecting electrical networks in the brain? It could be responsible for some of the tingling sensations as the brain gets vibrated over time.

However, I now know after more experience and study that the mantras are always working on all the levels. It's not about our experience of vibration but rather the fact that these are healing vibrations that help move us on our path of personal and spiritual growth. The vibrations begin to clear out old samskaras. However, as we begin to clear out old samskaras, this can take time.

My life has been full of drama and I have had a lot of samskaras to heal and clear out. Now, practicing TJY has brought me farther along on the path of healing. Even in the very beginning I noticed and felt profound changes and shifts for the better in dealing with personality complexes and life. And, I still needed to seek therapy with psychologists as a form of svadhyaya to help me find my way through my own psyche and emotions.

There are a lot of purely physical ways that chanting affects us. The cerebrospinal fluid flow is stimulated, the vagus nerve is stimulated, and the stress chemicals in the brain are reduced. More energy is felt simply because of these things. These are real physical things that are happening in the body as a result of chanting and meditation. Even just calm even breathing, done consciously, can have a positive effect on the mood, the vagus nerve and the cerebral spinal fluid flow. However, stress disrupts the flow of cerebral spinal fluid, and this has detrimental effects. Having good CSF flow is good for our vitality. Rhythmic, even breathing restores CSF flow.

Kundalini on the other hand is subtle energy. It can't be found in the physical realm. It exists in the spiritual realm as spiritual energy. (The same is also true of the chakras which may correspond to various organs in some ways, but are not the various organs themselves). However, although kundalini is spiritual energy, when it starts to wake up, it brings energy into the body and into the mind. Kundalini affects us. It is said that when kundalini makes it up to the head, things start to happen like third-eye opening, or various stages of awakening, that bring greater mental energy and clarity and insight. I know I have felt more energy mentally, since I have been feeling more energy from meditation, and a few times the light sensations going up into the head. I have experienced a leap in mental energy, and a return of creative energy. After kundalini activated in me, I have had mental clarity, greater than before, and began reading voluminously with good retention and learning, and having an easier time detaching from any drama I may encounter. I would not venture to say that my third-eye is totally open because I do not see auras and things like that; but it is definitely going through some sort of process and I feel sensations a lot now in the third-eye. I also experience heat and often break out into a little sweat near the end of my practice. Experiencing heat during meditation is a sign of active kundalini. Also, I recently experienced a kriya: I spontaneously sat up in bed, in the middle of sleep, and chanted a long sentence of Sanskrit mantra. After chanting the Sanskrit lines I laid back down into sleep. I didn't really fully wake up, and experienced myself from the inner-witness, as in a dream. Some part of my psyche seemed to be awake, observing what another part of my psyche was doing in sleep? Kriyas, or automatically performing yoga poses, pranayama, or Sanskrit chanting, are supposed to be a sign of kundalini activity.

Since it is subtle energy and it involves spiritual growth and evolution and we are all unique, there are not two experiences of kundalini unfolding that are alike, so we should avoid comparing and contrasting spiritual experiences. And still, there are some common things that we can see across the board that people start to experience: like experiences of energy; and, it is said that eventually everyone will experience an explosive rise of kundalini up into the crown chakra, resulting in a great opening of the mind, and causing us to use more parts of the brain that were unused before, giving us greater ability to conquer life's challenges.

When we are jivamukti or attained yet living, we still live day to day, live out the rest of our life, and we still have to deal with whatever life puts before us. We are here in the world and life goes on.

For me, I started to experience kundalini when I was resuming my TJY practices after almost a year of silence and therapy. At that time, I was practicing a long nyasa (chanting with sacred touching to divinize the body) that had a long part about the chakras in it; I also had been recovering from a blood clot that I got during my year off from chanting, so I was doing my practice lying down on the couch with my legs propped up on pillows, due to issues with circulation. I had just restarted and had done a few days of practice and then right away I started to experience kundalini energy; and since that time, now I always experience that energy when doing my TJY practice, sometimes more-so than others.

I do feel now that for the past two years, I have come to realize, that this is what is happening to me, that I'm living with activated kundalini that is working its way through my chakras. I can feel it.

I feel grateful for Pranashakti and Kundalini Shakti in my life. I feel grateful for the spiritual experiences that I have had because they have given me some insight into what the mind and the metaphysical are about, and if nothing else, they gave me food for thought, or pointed the way to the possibilities of other sorts of experiences and states of consciousness. In short, it gave me a sense of the mystical as tangible and real.

As for my part, I never consciously tried to awaken kundalini. I just took up the chanting to see what it was about and to find out what would happen to me if I pursued this path. I chanted with a feeling of reverence, and I think that is important. I remembered how I wept when chanting in the Lakshmi phase, wept like a baby on my mother's breast, sobbed and cried my heart out to Mother Lakshmi, and think she heard the prayers that sprang spontaneously from my heart in the midst of "just chanting." And mostly I just chanted, with as much awareness of what I was chanting as my brain could comfortably handle, without getting discursive, to have a feeling for what I was chanting about. In fact, Shajesh has commented more than once: "Just chant." One time, recently, when I told him about the light shooting up into my brow chakra, he said that was "good" and that I should not try to make it happen: "Just keep chanting," he said, and I just keep on doing my assignments, day after day.

It's very interesting to me how I had such a dry spell of creative energy and spiritual experience for years, after a serious trauma that caused PTSD, and other life stresses that followed, heaping on emotional wounds to heal. And now that I've been experiencing Kundalini energy, so much has come back to me: I feel my creative energy has returned and find myself finally writing a book, something I've wanted to do since graduate school.

I am 62 years old, and now I am starting to have spiritual experiences again: this time they are different – less like dreams and more like wide-awake experiences of energy in my chakras, and practical effects in my experience of living. Now, it seems I am more in the driver's seat. I just chant, or I just chant with images in mind related to the meaning of the mantra. Sometimes emotions or impressions enter into my mind; one can't stop to think about them and must just keep chanting. But occasionally one may become totally derailed by a strong emotion, such as happened to me recently: I just became so overcome with emotion, over the powerful and beautiful image of Devi's feet, embedded in what I was chanting about, that this huge emotion welled up in me and I collapsed in tears before the beautiful and powerful Devi, moved to a humble place of surrender. In moments like that, one should just let oneself cry, and let one's feelings go like prayer of the heart to the heart of the Divine, as I did in that moment, when tears overtook me; then resume chanting when it has passed. The mind is a vast, busy, and complex phenomenon and we can't suppress it into being still – we have to coax it little by little; if impressions enter into my mind, I just keep chanting. When one just continues to chant, the thoughts and emotions cycle through and become subdued. Just keeping the attention gently and consistently on the chanting is necessary.

As I have been experiencing this energy for the past two years, I have thoughts. My thoughts are that this energy – Kundalini Shakti – in my experience, is good and is very helpful. In my experience, the kundalini started to be active when my life started to calm down and when after years of therapy I was feeling more self-aware and integrated than before. Then, when my container was strong enough, I started to experience kundalini energy and in my experience it has felt healing and transformative.

The energy I experienced felt pleasant. Sometimes the energy would start to build and get a little intense, like a high pitch. The energy felt sort of like vibrational energy of some sort. I would start to chant and I would start to feel the energy about halfway through the practice. However at that time I only felt the energy when chanting, and for some reason at that time I was not chanting other mantras in between my daily practice for Shajesh. However, I have a host of mantras at my disposal and I probably was chanting one particular mantra, a form of Gayatri, on occasion, informally as I would go about my day.

In fact, I would characterize myself as a little lazy and haphazard when it comes to chanting. On the one hand I was very consistent in doing my assigned practices, and that consistency is a form of self-discipline. But, I didn't often have a regular meditation time of day. If there was a specific assignment, like the one I had to do before getting up out of bed in the morning, and I just sat there in the sheets, in my pajamas, chanting – that was a fairly regular time, because I tend to wake up around the same time each day. And when there was bedtime chanting to do, again that was more consistent as to a regular time.

I do tend to have a few different times of day and a couple of different locations that I chant in. So I am semi regular in my irregularity.

At the time I started to experience kundalini energy, I had been chanting laying down. Then, out of the blue, I started to feel I wanted to meditate sitting up to be sure I was having a straight spine and was more alert and I was hoping that sitting upright would facilitate my experience of the energy.

It was about a year ago now since I have started meditating sitting upright again. And I do enjoy it better. I sit with a lift under the hips – a meditation pillow – and it's advisable to have a little lift under the hips if one is sitting in sukhasana for meditation.

It was hard for me to return to sitting in sukhasana with a pillow under my hips, though I had sat that way in meditation for years. My hip got stiff from not sitting that way anymore, and it was hard for me. But I kept doing it and my hip opened up again. A person could certainly do meditation sitting in a chair, which doesn't work for me because when my legs hang down blood runs to my feet.

So the moral of this story is, if you are meditating and you want to just take your time and enjoy your life and unfold yourself in due time, relax, and don't fret the small things. Just keep doing your practice, whatever it is, and when the time is right for you, things will start to happen. Even when it seems nothing is happening, something is always happening on the inner layers.

I was meditating laying down for a while and I started to experience energy in a more obvious way. Then I started to meditate again sitting upright and I have continued to have energy experiences and a few times experienced a little rush of energy up into the head with a flash of light, which always seems to have an energizing effect. One time I experienced a rush of energy to the head with a flash of white light. Then the light faded and was followed by a rotating fractal pattern against a dark back-ground; so far that has only happened once, and I hear it is not about having spiritual experiences; it's about experiencing expanded consciousness – and awakening,

Spiritual experiences are like artifacts of meditation that show us we are on the path, evolving, but they are not the goal of practice. The goal of practice is awakening. Still and all, spiritual experiences gives us a sense of mystical realities, and should not be avoided, frowned upon, or devalued. Appreciate all your experiences, and be glad.

Conclusion:

Throughout my life I've had meaningful spiritual experiences, enigmatic happenings, and have pursued a variety of paths and practices. Finding Shajesh has been a real focal point of my spiritual pursuit. Practicing Tantric Japa Yoga for the past ten years has been a personal journey of unfolding and a study in a new paradigm – a new way of thinking – wherein I see myself as a microcosm of the macrocosm, on an interactive journey with the source of all creation, which lies mysteriously within me to be ever unfolded until I reach that final destination of moksha. Even if I achieved moksha, I would continue to live my life, learning as I go, so the process is never ending.

I'm grateful for the chance to explore this tradition that has brought me to a rich and still evolving sense of my own inner world and of the cosmos.

Meditation has been important to me, in one form or another, my whole life long, and Tantric Japa Yoga holds a significant place amid my lifetime of spiritual pursuit.

Tantric Japa Yoga has been an oral tradition passed down for generations from guru to teacher. Now these practices are open to you, so you too may enjoy and benefit!

Glossary

agni: the inner fire, or the fire element in Ayurveda, which governs digestion, and is necessary for life.

ahimsa: the principle of non-violence, which is one of the yamas.

ajna: the sixth chakra, located between the eyebrows in the center of the forehead.

anahata: the heart chakra, located in the center of the chest; also the unstruck sound.

anjali mudra: prayer gesture with palms pressed together in front of the heart and thumbs touching the sternum, which is the flat, vertical bone in the center of the chest.

antar mouna: a form of meditation that involves mindfully observing thoughts that arise spontaneously, with a detached awareness, discarding thoughts as they arise, eventually finding inner stillness, and the ability to maintain focus on a single thought, idea or image.

artha: is one of the four objectives of human life according to Hinduism, and entails finding ways to be prosperous financially through skills and career.

ascetic: a person who gives up worldly enjoyment and pursuits in favor of seeking God.

ashram: an ashram is a monestary in Hinduism and is a place of spiritual pilgrimage and retreat.

aura: the spiritual energy field surrounding a person's body, which is visible to some people.

awakening: awakening can happen slowly over time, as we evolve and grow spiritually, and as kundalini gets activated in our systems. Awakening as a term can be used to describe the process itself, or steps of insight and growth along the way, or can refer to the full, complete and final awakening known as kundalini awakening or final awakening, in which Shiva and Shakti unite in the crown and take up permanent residence there.

Ayurveda: an ancient holistic health science that is a sister science to yoga.

bhakti: worshipping a deity with love and devotion.

bhukti: worldly success and pleasure.

bija: a single-syllable sound or mantra which contains the vibration of the deity or element.

Brahma: a Hindu deity in charge of creating the universe, and who is part of the trinity of Brahma, Vishnu and Shiva.

Brahman: the ultimate reality underlying all creation and permeating throughout the phenomenal world.

chakras: energy centers in the body that organize our spiritual energy by focus and purpose, which process prana and ultimately kundalini, for the purpose of our spiritual unfoldment.

chidakasha: the blank space before the mind's eye or the dark space one sees when one closes one's eyes.

chidakasha dharana: a form of meditation in which one focuses one's attention on chidakasha and passively observes what arises there.

contemplation: looking at or considering something, such as an image imbued with feeling and meaning; viewing or being present to image, meaning and feeling, in a sustained way.

cosmology: a theory about the origin, nature and evolution of the universe.

dathus: seven categories of tissue function in the body, according to Ayurveda. In Tantra, there is a yogini associated with each dathu.

dakshina: an offering made to the guru or teacher by the student, in gratitude and respect for the role of the guru/teacher.

dharma: virtue, morality, and a sense of fulfilling one's worldly duties and living a righteous life.

dhyana: meditation and contemplation, as the mind resting in stable images, meaning and feeling, that flows.

discursive mind: the aspect of mind that thinks analytically and never stops chattering and worrying.

Diwali: festival of lights in India. Goddess Lakshmi is welcomed with worship and many lit candles to light her path.

dosha & subdosha: in Ayurveda there are three doshas which are body types and known as constitutions of a person's makeup. Subdoshas are categories of bodily functions that operate within the context of a specific dosha.

Durga: a very serious and powerful Hindu mother goddess who destroys demons and evil forces, and is a protector of humanity.

EMDR – a modern form of therapy that uses eye movements and tapping, as the client moves within. This form of therapy is used to treat trauma and PTSD.

enlightenment: a state of expanded consciousness achieved with the union of Shiva and Shakti in the crown.

Ganesh: the elephant headed deity who removes obstacles and who as om-incarnate, represents the evolutionary force in humanity.

Ganapathi: another name for Ganesh.

Gayatri Mantra: a Vedic prayer for enlightenment.

guru: a special teacher, and spiritual guide, who is seen as a manifestation of the divine, and who guides the aspirant on their path.

gurave: the guru within; one's own intelligence and self-awareness.

guru mantra: a special mantra that declares honor to the guru and invokes the power of the guru in the aspirant's sphere.

ham: a bija mantra associated with the throat/vishuddhi chakra and the ether element.

hridaya: the spiritual heart in Tantra, which is in some ways more expansive and all-encompassing than the heart chakra, anahata, and which is also a minor chakra a little bit lower than the heart chakra.

ida nadi: one of three main nadis that run through the chakras from bottom to top: the left or lunar channel, the feminine aspect, that ends in the left nostril.

inner-child work: this is a modern form of therapy in which the client imagines the inner-child and a wise, loving, parent. Through journaling and sometimes through drawing pictures or other methods, the interaction between the two is negotiated, yielding therapeutic results.

inner-witness: the function of the self that has the capacity to be self-aware.

japa: repeating a mantra over and over.

jivamukti: an enlightened soul, or one who has achieved liberation, kundalini-awakening, moksha, and is still living out their earthly life as such.

Kali: a very powerful mother goddess, often referred to as Kali-Ma, in Hinduism and in Tantra. Kali sprung from Durga's forehead when Durga was having trouble defeating the demons; Kali saved the day. She is a goddess of creation and destruction. When she is depicted with her right foot forward, she is in her function as creator. When her left foot is forward, she is in her function as destroyer. Kali is also "she who is greater than time" – the goddess of time.

kama: desire, enjoyment, attraction, and pleasure.

kapalbhati: a pranayama or breathing exercise in which the belly is pumped in forcefully and repeatedly on the exhale, while the inhale is passive.

kapha: one of three doshas or body types of Ayurveda, kapha is associated with the earth and water elements.

karma: the law of cause and effect, which explains that our actions have consequences.

kriya: a yoga posture, breath-work, or Sanskrit chanting, that is performed spontaneously, often in the middle of sleep, as a result of kundalini activity in the body.

kundalini: a latent, divine feminine energy – the static ground of our being, that holds us in incarnation in our bodies – that is located at the base of the spine in the muladhara chakra, and when activated rises up through sushumna chakra, making its way through each of the chakras one by one, until finally uniting permanently with Shiva in the crown, creating enlightenment.

kundalini activation – kundalini can be active within a person but still may not have risen all the way to the crown and stayed there for full kundalini awakening.

kundalini awakening: final culmination of kundalini rising, or final union of Shiva and Shakti in the crown.

Kundalini Shakti: Goddess Shakti in Her aspect as Kundalini.

lam: a bija mantra associated with the base/muladhara chakra, and the earth element.

Lakshmi: an auspicious and very important Goddess who cares about our success in life.

Maha Shivaratri: a yearly festival on the dark of the moon, in which participants stay up all night and worship Lord Shiva with chanting, dancing and other rituals, to invite and greet the new light of the morning, celebrating the triumph of light over dark. Maha Shivaratri means the great night of Shiva. Maha means great, and ratri means night.

manipura: known as the solar plexus, this is the chakra below the rib cage and above the belly button, and is associated with one's social self.

marma: a system of pressure points in Ayurveda, that can be used for healing.

matrika: the letters of the Sanskrit alphabet, each of which are distinct shaktis or energy vibrations.

matrika nyasa: a practice of divinizing the body by placing the letters of the Sanskrit alphabet (matrika), one by one, on various locations of the body.

maya: maya is the illusory nature of our world. Maya is an aspect of Goddess Shakti, and she is responsible for veiling the ultimate reality. It's not that the physical world is not real, but that the deeper reality is veiled so that the surface reality that we see is illusory, not because it isn't real, but because its true nature and inner core reality are veiled.

meditation: a practice that calms the mind and improves energy, giving a sense of well-being, and leading to moksha.

moksha: spiritual liberation; liberation from the cycle of death and rebirth.

monkey-mind: the discursive mind is often referred to as the monkey mind because it never knows when to settle down, and always is busy analyzing, ruminating, and worrying about all sorts of things.

mudra: hand gestures that express a spiritual intention and activate certain energies.

mukti: spiritual liberation

muladhara: the base or root chakra, at the base of the spine, where kundalini resides, and which is related to our sense of safety and belonging in the world.

nada: the original sound/vibration, that is very subtle and is related to the om vibration.

nadi shodhana/nadi shuddhi: a pranayama or breath-work otherwise known as alternate nostril breathing.

nadi: an energy pathway in the body: there are 72,000 nadis in the human body. Most nadis carry prana; but sushumna nadi or the central channel carries only kundalini.

namaste: a greeting which acknowledges our common ground of being.

nirguna: the formless aspect of a deity.

niyamas: positive things we should do in order to live a spiritual life.

nyasa: a practice of divinizing the body by placing mantras at various places on the body with a special mudra.

ojas: the subtle aspect of the water element in Ayurveda, which is related to certain aspects of bodily function.

Om: the original vibration, the original sound, the original word, and the infinite beyond conception, from which all creation sprang.

Parvati: in Hinduism and Tantra Parvati is the original wife of Lord Shiva in myth and Story. Parvati is one of many names for Goddess Shakti.

pancha maha bhutas: the five elements of creation, namely: earth, water, fire, air, and ether.

pingala nadi: one of three main nadis that run through the chakras from bottom to top: the masculine or solar aspect, that ends in the right nostril.

pitta: one of three doshas or body types in Ayurveda, pitta is associated with the fire element.

prana: life force energy and a form of goddess Shakti, closely related to the breath. Also, the subtle aspect of vata, the air element, in Ayurveda, which is related to certain bodily functions.

pranafied: infused and charged up with prana.

Pranashakti: Goddess Shakti in Her form as Prana or life force energy.

pranayama: a conscious breathing exercise.

ram: a bija mantra associated with the solar plexus or manipura chakra and the fire element.

reincarnation: the rebirth of souls, to live one lifetime after another.

rishis: enlightened ones who were inspired by divine revelation and transmitted knowledge to humanity. Lord Shiva taught Parvati directly, then Parvati taught to the rishis, who learned in states of deep meditation.

sadhaka: a person who follows a particular spiritual practice.

sadhana: a disciplined practice that is intended to progress one along the spiritual path.

sadhu: a spiritual ascetic or holy person.

saguna: the aspect of the deity that has a visual form associated with it; the visual form of the deity typically has symbolic aspects and points in the direction of the nirguna or formless aspect of the deity.

sahasrara: known as the crown chakra, located in the top of the head, sahasrara chakra is our spiritual center and is responsible for our sense of connection to divinity.

samadhi: a blissful feeling one gets after meditating. There are various stages of samadhi, and samadhi that is achieved with enlightenment is said to never end.

samskara: programming and imprints in our psyche from past experiences or trauma.

sankalpa: a resolve or intention one may set to define the mood of one's meditation or practice.

satsang: a gathering of spiritual people for the purpose of spiritual practice and/or instruction.

Savitur: a solar deity who is the light of the pre-dawn sun.

Shakti: the feminine aspect of creation in tantric cosmology, who is considered to be energy.

shaktipat: divine transmission from the guru to the student. The guru transmits divine spiritual energy which is the Divine Mother, directly to the student.

Shodashi: the chief goddess of Sri Vidya, also known as Sri Maha Tripurasundari.

Shiva: the masculine aspect of creation in Tantric cosmology, who is considered to be consciousness.

siddhi: a magical power attained through spiritual practice.

spanda: the primal pulse or vibration of consciousness, energy, and being.

Sri Bala Tripurasundari: the child goddess, who is the nine-year-old daughter of Tripurasundari.

Sri Mata: the Great Mother

Sri Maha Tripurasundari: the chief goddess of Sri Vidya, who is the original explosion of creation from consciousness and energy, and who is the consort to Lord Shiva.

Sri Vidya: the study of Sri Mata or the Great Mother; a study of a group of individual goddesses each representing her own archetypal force, culminating in Tripurasundari, also known as Shodashi.

sukhasana: sweet pose, or a comfortable easy sitting position, usually means sitting cross-legged.

subtle body: sometimes referred to as the energy body, the subtle body is energetic rather than physical.

sushumna nadi: the central channel; the main nadi that runs in a straight line up from the base chakra to the crown chakra, and which is reserved solely for Kundalini Shakti.

svadhyaya: self-study, or study of sacred scriptures.

swadhisthana: the second chakra located in the lower belly, below the belly button, and which relates to our emotional, creative, and sexual energy.

tandava: a dance that Lord Shiva dances, through the processes of creation, preservation, and destruction of the universe.

tapas: the heat of spiritual practice, or results that come from our effort.

tarpanam: a ritual of water offering to a deity, in which specific Sanskrit mantras are chanted throughout, as water is poured/offered from the hands over the deity.

tejas: according to Ayurveda, the subtle essence of pitta dosha or the fire element in the body that creates heat and luster in the body; the inner fire; the inner sun.

third-eye: another name for ajna chakra, which is located between the eye-brows in the center of the forehead. The two physical eyes are associated with external sight; while the third-eye is associated with inner sight or intuition.

trataka: a form of meditation that entails gazing at a fixed point of focus, often at the flame of a candle.

tulsi: the sacred holy basil plant which is associated with the Goddess Lakshmi.

Ultimate Reality: or "the Ultimate," a term that refers to the nirguna aspect of God, which is formless and beyond our comprehension.

Vak: the goddess of speech.

vam: a bija mantra associated with the swadhisthana chakra and the water element.

vata: one of three doshas or body types in Ayurveda, vata is associated with the air element.

Vedas: sacred spiritual texts revealed through divine revelation, first orally transmitted then written down.

vishuddhi: the throat chakra, located in the center of the throat, and related to our self-expression.

vyahritis: the three worlds mentioned at the start of the Gayatri Mantra: bhur, bhuva, swah. There are actually seven vyahrities. However the three at the start of the Gayatri Mantra are the primary vyahritis.

yam: a bija mantra associated with the heart chakra, anahata, and with the air element.

yamas: a set of ethical guidelines on how to live a spiritual life.

yantra: a geometric design that is considered to embody the energy and essence of the deity.

Bibliography

Acharya, Shriram Sharma, *Super Science of Gayatri,*
Reprint. Yug Nirman Yojana Vistar Trust, 2019.

Arundale, G.S., *Kundalini: An Occult Experience*, Second
Ed., Second Reprint, Theosophical Publishing House,
2019

Avalon, Arthur (Sir John Woodroffe), *The Serpent Power:
The Secrets of Tantric & Shaktic Yoga*, Seventh Ed.,
Republished, Dover Publications 1974.

Bandyapadhyay, Pranab, *The Goddess of Tantra*, Second Ed.,
Reprint, P.K. Bhattacharya Punthi Pustak, Publishers,
2002

Bhanudas, H.H.Shrimad Naamchaitanya, *Unique Insights
Into The Gayatri Mantra*, Aanjaneya Dhananjay
Dhawale, 2013.

Baeumer, Bettina Sharada, *The Yoga of Netra Tantra: Third
Eye and Overcoming Death*, The Secretary Indian
Institute of Advanced Study, and, D.K. Printworld
Ltd., 2019.

'Chaitanya,' J. L. Gupta, *The Healing Power of Yoga & Kundalini Tantra: Path to Wellness & Enlightenment*, Penman Publishers, 2010.

Chidananda, Swami, *God as Mother*, Sixth Ed., Swami Vimalananda for the Divine Life Society, 2006.

Dev OM, T*he Cosmic Energy & Chakras*, Om Foundation, 2nd. Ed., 2015

Dudeja, Prof. (Dr.) Jai Paul, Om *Namah Shivaya: A Powerful Mantra for Mastering Five Elements*, Notion Press, 2022.

Dudeja, Prof. (Dr.) Jai Paul Dudeja, *Quantum Science of Ganesha Consciousness*, Notion Press, 2022.

Dudeja, Prof. (Dr.) Jai Paul, *The Third-eye: A Spiritual Laser for Stimulating Inner Awakening*, Gen Next Publication, 2019.

Greenwell, Bonnie, Ph.D., *The Kundalini Guide: A Companion for the Inward Journey*, Shakti River Press, 2014.

Gupta, Sanjukta, *Lakshmi Tantra: A Pancaratra Text*, Reprint, First Ed., Motilal Banarsidass Publishers, 2007.

Harshananda, Swami, *Siva and Ganapati*, Second Ed., Swami Harshananda, 2000.

Hughes, John, Ed., Shiva Sutras: The Supreme Awakening
(with Ksemaraja's Commentary), Third Ed.,
Lakshmanjoo Academy, 2015.

Johari, Harish, *Chakras: Energy Centers of Transformation*,
Destiny Books, 2000.

Jyotirmayananda, Swami, Mantra Shiromani: *The Crest-
Jewels of Mantra, Gayatri and Mahamityunjaya
Mantras*, Yoga Research Foundation, 2017.

Kinsley, David, *Tantric Visions of the Divine Feminine: The
Ten MahaVidyas*, University of California Press,
1997.

Krishna, Gopi, *Kundalini: The Evolutionary Energy in Man,
with Psychological Commentary by James Hillman*,
Shambala, 1997.

Kumar, Prof. Ravindra, Ph.D. (Swami Atmananda),
Kundalini for Beginners, Sterling Paperbacks, 2018.

Kumar, Dr. Ravindra (Dr. Swami Ravindraanandh), *The
Shortest Path of Self-Realization: Secrets of Divine
Grace Awakening of KUNDALINI))*, First Indian
Edition, Motilal Banarsidass Publishing House, 2022.

Mukhyananda, Svami, Om *Gayatri and Sandhya*, Adhyaksha
Sri Ramakrishna Math, 2014.Muller-Ortega, Paul
Eduardo, *The Triadic Heart of Siva: Kaula
Tantricism of Abhinavagupta in the Non-Dual
Shaivism of Kashmir*, State University of New York
Press, 1989.

Muni, Rajarsi, *Yoga Experiences, Part-I,* First, Ed., Shri
Dayabhai Hirabhai Patel, 1977.

Navaratnam, Ratna Ma, Om *Tat Sat: The Call of Maha Sakti
Mother Divine*, Bharatiya Vidya Bhavan, 1993.

Omkarananda, Paramahamsa, *The Divine Mother*, Edited by
S. Vidyaprakashananda, First Ed., Motilal
Banarsidass Publishers,
2019.

Panda, N.C., *Japa Yoga (Mantra-Yoga): Theory, Practice
and Applications*, D.K. Printworld (P) Ltd., 2007.

Panda, N.C. *Mind & Supermind, Vol. I,* D.K. Printworld (P)
Ltd., 1994.

Panda, N.D., *Yoga-Nidra (Yogic Trance): Theory, Practice
And Applications*, Third Impression, D.K. Printworld
(P) Ltd.2018.

Pathar, M.A., L.T., S. Viraswami, *Gayatri Mantra*, Sura
College of Competition, First Ed., 2015.

Pattanaik, Devdutt, *Lakshmi: The Goddess of Wealth and Fortune, An Introduction,* Vakils, Feffer and Simons Pvt. Ltd, 2002.

Perring H.B., Michael 'omdevaji,' *A Pocket Book on Kundalini:The 'What on Earth is Kundalini?' Series – Book IV*, Pilgrims Publishing, 2015.

Rao, Dr. P.J. Mohana, *Meditation of Sun in Heart: Aditya Hridayam*, Agasthya Publications, Second Ed., 2023.

Ramamurthy N., Dr., *Sri Tripurasundari Devi,* Pub'd at Chennai, First Ed., 2022.

Rhodes, Constantina, *Invoking Lakshmi: The Goddess of Wealth in Song and Ceremony*, Suny Press, 2010.

Saraswati, Swami Dayananda, *Prayer Guide (with explanations of several Mantras, Stotras, Kirtans, and Religious Festivals)*, First Ed., Arsha Vidya Centre, 2008.

Saraswati, Swami Niranjanananda, *Prana Pranayama Prana Vidya*, Second Ed., Bihar School of Yoga, 2002

Saraswati, Swami Satyananda, *Ganesa Puja*, Second Ed., Devi Mandir Publications, 2001.

Saraswati, Swami Satyananda, *Kundalini Tantra*, Bihar School of Yoga, 1984.

Singh, Jaideva, *Abhinavagupta Paratrisika Vivarana: The Secret of Tantric Mysticism*, 8th Reprint, Motilal Banarsidass, 2017.

Sivananda, Swami, *Lord Siva and His Worship*, The Divine Life Society, 2008.

Srikant, *Alphabet of Reality Series, Significance of Divine Forms: Sri Ganesa*, First Ed., Integral Books, 2015.

Svatantranandanatha, Siddha Sri, *Sri Matrkacakra Vivekah: Mantra sastra of Kasmira, revealing secrets of Mantra's origins and their meaning on the basis of matrka inscribed Sri Yantra called Matrka Cakra*, Translated by G. Mishra,First Ed., Chaukhamba Surbharati Prakashan, 2016.
2016.

Torrey, R. A., *Hall of Faith Classics Volume 1: The Person and Work of the Holy Spirit as Revealed in the Scriptures and in Personal Experience*, G.I.L. Publications.com, 1910.

Vanamali, *Sri Devi Lila: The Play of the Divine Mother,* Aryan Books International, 2006.

Varshney, Mrs. Madhu, Comp., *Shiva-Shakti Aaraadhanaa*,
Richa Prakashan, n.d. Ramamurthy N., Dr.*Sri Tripura
Sundari Devi*,Dr. Ramamurthy N., 2022.

Rao, Dr. P.J. Mohana, *Meditation of Sun in Heart:
Aditya Hirdayam*, Agastya Publicationsm, Second
Ed., 2023.

Wolf, Fred Alan, Ph.D., *the dreaming universe: a mind
expanding journey into the realm where psyche and
physics meet,* Simon & Schuster, 1994.

Wolf, Fred Alan, Ph.D., *The Spiritual Universe: One
Physicist's Vision of Spirit, Soul, Mater, and Self,*
Moment Point Press, 2nd Ed., 1999.

Index